THE
EVERYTHING®
French Grammar Book

Dear Reader,

I am pleased to be able to share my love and knowledge of the French language with you. Since 1999, I've
been teaching French via the Internet (About the French
Language—*http://french.about.com*) and it's thanks to this
Web site that I am now writing books.

   When I was studying French, I was utterly baffled by
some of the grammatical constructions I was supposed
to memorize. I thought that I would never be able to
remember them, and certainly not be able to speak French
with anything approaching the ease with which I speak
English. But now I can, and I am sure that one day you will
be able to as well.

   Bon courage !

   Laura K. Lawless

The EVERYTHING Series

Editorial

Publishing Director	Gary M. Krebs
Director of Product Development	Paula Munier
Associate Managing Editor	Laura M. Daly
Associate Copy Chief	Brett Palana-Shanahan
Acquisitions Editor	Gina Chaimanis
Development Editor	Rachel Engelson
Associate Production Editor	Casey Ebert

Production

Director of Manufacturing	Susan Beale
Associate Director of Production	Michelle Roy Kelly
Cover Design	Paul Beatrice
	Matt LeBlanc
	Erick DaCosta
Design and Layout	Colleen Cunningham
	Sorae Lee
	Jennifer Oliveira
Series Cover Artist	Barry Littmann

Visit the entire Everything® Series at *www.everything.com*

THE
EVERYTHING®
FRENCH
GRAMMAR
BOOK

All the rules you need to master français

Laura K. Lawless

Adams Media
Avon, Massachusetts

À tous mes professeurs de français : merci beaucoup !

• • •

An Everything® Series Book.
Everything® and everything.com® are
registered trademarks of F+W Publications, Inc.

Published by Adams Media, an F+W Publications Company
57 Littlefield Street, Avon, MA 02322 U.S.A.
www.adamsmedia.com

ISBN: 1-59337-528-X

Printed in The United States of America.

J I H G F E D C B A

Library of Congress Cataloging-in-Publication Data
Lawless, Laura K.
The everything French grammar book / Laura K. Lawless.
p. cm. -- (The everything series)
Includes bibliographical references.
ISBN 1-59337-528-X
1. French language--Grammar. 2. French language--Textbooks
for foreign speakers--English. I. Title. II. Series.

PC2112.L36 2006
448.2'421--dc22

2006005011

This book is available at quantity discounts for bulk purchases.
For information, please call 1-800-872-5627

Contents

Acknowledgments

As always I must thank my wonderful agent, Barb Doyen, for her support. I'd also like to say *merci* to my editor, Gina Chaimanis, and all of the folks at Adams Media who helped to create this book. Above all, I want to thank all of my French teachers, who did their best to not only teach me French, but show me the beauty and logic of the language. If I had known then what I know now, maybe I wouldn't have been so difficult in French class. *Je vous remercie.*

Introduction

BIENVENUE AND WELCOME to the wonderful world of French. Grammar is not the most exciting part of language learning, but it is beautiful in its own way. There is always logic involved in the various constructions; the problem is that this logic is specific to each language—what is logical in French may not be so in English, and vice versa.

The best way to learn another language is to try to avoid comparing everything to your own language, and above all not asking "why?" When you are further along in your studies, it can be very interesting to ask why something is said a certain way, but in the beginning, the explanations are likely to be either unhelpful or downright confusing.

Right now, just try to understand the various constructions and how to use them. When it seems overwhelming, remember why you want to learn French—to travel, get a job overseas, or chat with French speakers who live nearby. Having a goal in mind can be a great source of inspiration in your studies. As you develop fluency, you will need to think about how to say what you want to say less and less, and this too can be very inspiring.

Your interest in this book means that you are either looking to learn French grammar or build on what you've already learned. Either way, you will find that this book has just what you need: lessons that are detailed without being overwhelming; tips and tricks to help you remember difficult points, distinguish between similar words, and avoid pitfalls; and *Exercices de contrôle* at the end of each chapter to make sure you understand the lessons.

At the end of the book, you'll find verb tables for sample verbs and the most common irregular verbs. These verb tables only include simple (single verb) conjugations. This is because compound (double verb) conjugations are based on simple conjugations and are very easy to figure out, so there is no need to conjugate hundreds of verbs into another seven tenses. If you study the verb lessons in this book, you should have no trouble conjugating the compound tenses.

So without further ado, look to the next page and start learning about French grammar.

Chapter 1

Introduction to French

LEARNING FRENCH IS not the easiest thing in the world, but it can be extremely interesting and worthwhile. Whether you want to visit French-speaking countries, chat with native speakers who live nearby, or just learn more about the world, being able to speak French well will definitely make the experience more enjoyable.

French Language Classification

French is a Romance language, although that's not why it's called the language of love. In linguistic terms, "Romance" comes from the word Roman and simply means "from Latin." The complete language family classification of French is Indo-European > Italic > Romance. Here are some things to know about the language classification of French:

- Indo-European is the largest language family and contains most European, American, and Asian languages, including Latin, Greek, Gaelic, Polish, and Hindi.
- Italic basically refers to Latin.
- Romance languages are originally from Western Europe, although due to colonization, some of them are found all over the world. French, Spanish, Italian, and Portuguese are all Romance languages.

Since Romance languages are all descended from Latin, they tend to be similar in many ways to one another. If you have already studied another Romance language, you will find that some French concepts are very easy for you because you already learned about them when studying a previous language.

 *Question?*

How does the classification of English compare to that of French?
The classification of English is Indo-European > Germanic > Western.

French Speakers

French is an official language in dozens of countries as well as in numerous immigrant communities in the United States and around the world. French is the second most commonly taught second language in the world, after English. French is the official language in:

- Benin
- Burkina Faso
- Central African Republic
- Ivory Coast
- Democratic Republic of Congo (formerly Zaïre)
- France and its overseas territories
- Gabon
- Geneva, Jura, Neuchâtel, and Vaud (Swiss districts)
- Guinea
- Luxembourg
- Mali
- Monaco
- Niger
- Quebec (Canadian province)
- Republic of the Congo
- Senegal
- Togo

French is one of two or more official languages in Belgium, Burundi, Cameroon, Canada, Chad, Comoros Islands, Djibouti, Equatorial Guinea, Haiti, Madagascar, Rwanda, Seychelles, Switzerland, and Vanuatu.

French is also important, though not the official language, in a number of other countries. Whether as an administrative, commercial, or international language, or due to the reality of a considerable French-speaking population, French is also found in Algeria, Andorra, Argentina, Brazil, Cambodia, Cape Verde, Dominica, Egypt, Greece, Grenada, Guinea-Bissau, India, Italy (Valle d'Aosta), Laos, Lebanon, Mauritania, Mauritius, Morocco, Poland, Syria, Trinidad and Tobago, Tunisia, United Kingdom (Channel Islands), United States (Louisiana, New England), Vatican City, and Vietnam.

All in all, in 1999, French was the 11th most common first language in the world, though the number of speakers is a little difficult to pin down. According to the *Ethnologue Report*, there are 77 million first language speakers and 51 million second language speakers. The *Rapport sur l'état de la Francophonie dans le monde* breaks the figures down a little differently, with 113 million Francophones (people who speak French fluently and regularly), 61 million "occasional" Francophones (who live in a francophone country but do not speak French regularly), and about 100 million students of French.

French is the third most frequently spoken non-English language in U.S. homes (after Spanish and Portuguese) and the second most commonly taught foreign language in the United States (after Spanish).

 Fact

The word *Francophonie* refers to both the phenomenon of speaking French and the French-speaking community. From this word, there is an adjective, *francophone* (French-speaking), and a noun, *un/une francophone* (a French speaker).

There are numerous variations in grammar, vocabulary, and pronunciation both between and within French-speaking regions. This means that there may be some confusion when you talk to French speakers from different countries, but you should be able to communicate with Francophones wherever you go without too much difficulty, even if the French you learned is from another region.

French in English

French has had a great deal of influence on English, affecting English grammar, vocabulary, and pronunciation. The French influence on English began in 1066, when William the Conqueror led the Norman invasion of England and became King of England.

While English was relegated to the language of the masses, French became the language of the court, administration, and culture and would remain that way for 300 years. French and English thus co-existed with no apparent complications; in fact, English was essentially ignored by grammarians during this time and evolved into a grammatically simpler language. After just 70 or 80 years of this peaceful co-existence, Old English became Middle English.

Vocabulary

As a result of the Norman occupation of England, English adopted about 10,000 French words, of which around three-fourths are still used today. This vocabulary is found in every domain: art, literature, cuisine, government, and law. More than a third of all English words are derived from French, either directly or indirectly. An English speaker who has never studied French already knows around 15,000 French words!

Pronunciation

English pronunciation was also affected by French. Old English had the unvoiced fricative sounds *f* as in "fat," *s* as in "same," *sh* as in "shin," and the *th* as in "thin," and French helped to distinguish the voiced sounds *v* as in "vote," *z* as in "zone," and *zh* as in "mirage." French also contributed the diphthong *oy* as in "boy."

 **Essential**

> "Fricative" indicates that passage of air is partially blocked in pro-
> nouncing a sound. "Voiced" sounds are those that are pronounced
> with vibrating vocal cords, while "unvoiced" sounds do not cause the
> vocal cords to vibrate.

Grammar

French had much less influence on English grammar, but you can see a few elements of French grammar in the English language. One notable example is found in the word order of expressions like "attorney general" and "surgeon general," where English uses noun + adjective, which is typical of French, rather than the normal English word order of adjective + noun.

Why Learn French?

There are numerous reasons to learn a foreign language in general, and French in particular. One reason is that French is the *lingua franca* of culture, including art, cuisine, dance, and fashion. France has won more Nobel Prizes for literature than any other country in the world and is one of the top producers of international films.

French is an official working language in dozens of international organizations, including the United Nations, International Olympic Committee, and International Red Cross. French is also the second most frequently used language on the Internet, and is ranked the second most influential language in the world.

Communication and Cultural Understanding

An obvious reason to learn a new language is to be able to communicate with the people who speak it, such as people you meet when traveling or perhaps even people in your own community. Speaking another language helps you understand another culture.

Language defines and is defined by the people who speak it, thus learning another language helps you understand new ideas and new ways of looking at the world.

Speaking another language also allows you to enjoy literature, film, and music in the original language. A translation can never be 100 percent faithful to the original, so the best way to understand what the author or filmmaker really meant is to read or watch what the artist actually created.

Business and Careers

Fluency in more than one language will increase your market-ability and can make it easier for you to get a job. Many schools and employers give preference to candidates who speak one or more foreign languages. While English is spoken throughout much of the world, it is not the only language, and many companies prefer to use their own language whenever possible. When dealing with a client in France, for example, a French speaker will have an obvious advantage over someone who doesn't speak French.

Language Enhancement

When you learn another language, you discover many aspects about your native language that you were previously unaware of. English has developed over hundreds of years, thanks in large part to the contributions of many other languages. Learning a language like French, German, or Latin will teach you where words and even grammatical structures are from, as well as increase your vocabulary.

Language is very often an instinctive skill—you know how to speak, but you may not always be able to explain why you say something one way rather than another. Learning a new language can help you understand the rules behind what you instinctively know how to say.

Each additional language you study will tend to be a little easier, as you get used to the particular skills needed to learn another language. Plus, when you learn related languages, such as French and

Spanish, Swedish and Danish, or Russian and Polish, there will be many similarities between the two languages, which makes learning the second one that much easier.

 Fact

Although English is a Germanic language and not a Romance language like French, French has had an enormous impact on English vocabulary. In fact, French is the largest donor of foreign words in English, so learning French will increase the number of English words you know.

Test Scores

Math and verbal SAT scores increase with years of foreign language study, according to the Admissions Testing Program of the College Board. Children who study a foreign language tend to have higher standardized test scores, and foreign language study can help to increase problem-solving skills, memory, and self-discipline.

True Cognates

One of the main components of language learning is vocabulary—memorizing the thousands of words that you need to talk about the world around you. For English speakers, one of the nice things about learning French is that there are some shortcuts you can take when learning vocabulary. For example, there are hundreds of true cognates—words which look similar in the two languages and have the same or similar meanings. These are nearly always nouns or adjectives. The following table lists a few of the most important ones.

True Cognates

MASCULINE NOUNS	FEMININE NOUNS	ADJECTIVES
abandon	absence	absent
accent	action	brave
accident	architecture	central
agent	automobile	certain
air	avenue	civil
angle	calorie	correct
animal	cassette	dental
art	cause	exact
article	cigarette	excellent
client	condition	final
cousin	description	fragile
danger	destination	horrible
dessert	distance	impossible
effort	excuse	long
film	finance	musical
fruit	fortune	partial
garage	image	public
million	machine	simple
respect	nation	six
saint	olive	unique
service	question	urgent
ski	radio	vacant
taxi	situation	violet

There are thousands of cognates between French and English, but they are not always true. Always check a dictionary or ask a native speaker before assuming that similar words mean the same thing.

False Cognates

Although the preceding section can be very helpful, don't let it lull you into a false sense of security. Not all words that look alike mean the same thing—there are also hundreds of false cognates: words that look alike but have different meanings. There are also many semi-false cognates; that is, words which have several meanings, only some of which are similar in the two languages. The following table of some of the most common false and semi-false cognates will give you a good starting point for some serious work with a dictionary.

Common false and semi-false cognates

Actuellement vs Actually	*Assister* vs Assist
Attendre vs Attend	*Avertissement* vs Advertisement
Blesser vs Bless	*Bras* vs Bras
Caractère vs Character	*Cent* vs Cent
Chair vs Chair	*Chance* vs Chance
Christian vs Christian	*Coin* vs Coin
Collège vs College	*Commander* vs Command
Con vs Con	*Crayon* vs Crayon
Déception vs Deception	*Demander* vs Demand
Déranger vs Derange	*Douche* vs Douche
Entrée vs Entrée	*Envie* vs Envy
Éventuellement vs Eventually	*Expérience* vs Experience
Finalement vs Finally	*Football* vs Football
Formidable vs Formidable	*Gentil* vs Gentle
Gratuité vs Gratuity	*Gros* vs Gross
Ignorer vs Ignore	*Librairie* vs Library
Occasion vs Occasion	*Opportunité* vs Opportunity
Parti/Partie vs Party	*Pièce* vs Piece
Professeur vs Professor	*Publicité* vs Publicity
Quitter vs Quit	*Raisin* vs Raisin
Rater vs Rate	*Réaliser* vs Realize
Rester vs Rest	*Réunion* vs Reunion
Robe vs Robe	*Sale* vs Sale
Sympathique vs Sympathetic	*Type* vs Type
Unique vs Unique	*Zone* vs Zone

There are hundreds of false cognates and there are hundreds of true cognates. The bottom line is that you just need to be careful—if a French word looks a lot like an English one, it might mean the same thing, but it might not. Look it up in the dictionary just to be on the safe side!

Chapter 2

Nouns and Articles

IN THIS CHAPTER you will learn about French nouns and articles, two separate but interdependent parts of speech. The term "part of speech" refers to the grammatical classification of the function or purpose of a word. All words can be categorized into one of nine parts of speech: nouns, articles, adjectives, pronouns, verbs, adverbs, prepositions, conjunctions, and interjections. The other parts of speech will be discussed in later chapters.

Introduction to Nouns

A noun is a word that represents a thing, either concrete (e.g., a chair, a doctor) or abstract (life, love). Traditionally a noun is defined as a "person, place, or thing," but that description is sometimes considered too limiting, and therefore "idea" and/or "quality" are sometimes added to the definition. Regular nouns, also known as "common nouns," are just that: teacher, city, war, and so on. "Proper nouns" are the names of specific persons, places, or events and are usually capitalized, such as Laura, Paris, and World War II.

The most important thing to know about French nouns is that each one has a gender—either masculine or feminine. The gender of some nouns makes sense: *homme* (man) is masculine, *femme* (woman) is feminine, but others don't: *personne* (person) is always feminine, even if the person is a male, and *livre* (book) is masculine even though a book is no more like a man than a woman.

Essential

> For English speakers, grammatical gender may seem totally illogical, but it's just part of the language. Trying to figure out why a word is masculine or feminine will just frustrate you; you're better off learning words with their gender and not worrying about why.

It is very important to learn a French noun's gender along with the noun itself because articles, adjectives, and some verbs have to agree with nouns; that is, they change according to the gender of the noun they modify. The best way to learn the gender of nouns is to make your vocabulary lists with the definite or indefinite article. That is, instead of making a list like this:

homme	man
femme	woman
garçon	boy
fille	girl

You should make your list like this, so that you learn the gender along with the word:

un homme	man
une femme	woman
un garçon	boy
une fille	girl

In other words, the gender is part of the word. Think of the French word for man not as *homme* but rather as *homme (m)* or: (un) homme. Make the effort to learn each word with its gender now, while you are beginning to learn French. If you don't, you may find yourself looking in the dictionary every five minutes even after you are no longer a novice French speaker, trying to determine the gender of hundreds of nouns that you did not learn correctly when you started learning French.

Many people beginning to learn French wonder if gender really matters when it comes to being understood by another French speaker. The answer is, yes. Many nouns have only a masculine or feminine form, so using the wrong gender would be like mispronouncing the word—it would be a mistake but you would probably still be understood. However, there are a number of nouns that are pronounced the same way but have different meanings depending on whether they are masculine or feminine, so using the wrong gender would mean you were saying a different word. The bottom line: gender matters.

Gender and Number of Nouns

One of the characteristics of nouns is that they may have up to four different forms, depending on their gender and number. Most English nouns have a singular and plural form (book, books), and the same is true for most French nouns (*livre, livres*). In addition, some nouns have different forms for masculine and feminine: some English nouns that refer to people (waiter, waitress) and animals (lion, lioness) and most French nouns that refer to people (*serveur, serveuse*) and some that indicate animals (*lion, lionne*). Thus there are up to four possible forms for each noun: masculine singular (waiter, *serveur*), feminine singular (waitress, *serveuse*), masculine plural (waiters, *serveurs*), and feminine plural (waitresses, *serveuses*). Fortunately, the rules for making French nouns plural and/or feminine are fairly straightforward.

Most nouns add an *e* for feminine and an *s* for plural.

UN AMI (FRIEND)

	singular	plural
masculine	ami	amis
feminine	amie	amies

UN COUSIN (COUSIN)

	singular	plural
masculine	cousin	cousins
feminine	cousine	cousines

When a masculine noun ends in an unaccented e, there is no difference between the masculine and feminine forms.

UN TOURISTE (TOURIST)

	singular	plural
masculine	touriste	touristes
feminine	touriste	touristes

UN ARTISTE (ARTIST)

	singular	plural
masculine	artiste	artistes
feminine	artiste	artistes

When a noun ends in s, x, or z there is no difference between the singular and plural forms.

	SINGULAR	PLURAL
son	le fils	les fils
price	le prix	les prix
gas	le gaz	les gaz

The above rules cover the majority of French nouns, but there are also some irregular gender patterns.

ENDING	MASCULINE NOUN	FEMININE ENDING	FEMININE NOUN
-an	paysan	-anne	paysanne
-en	gardien	-enne	gardienne
-er	boulanger	-ère	boulangère
-eur	danseur	-euse	danseuse
-on	patron	-onne	patronne
-teur	acteur	-trice	actrice

There are also some irregular plural patterns.

ENDING	SINGULAR	PLURAL ENDING	PLURAL NOUN
-ail	*travail*	-aux	*travaux*
-al	*cheval*	-aux	*chevaux*
-eau	*château*	-eaux	*châteaux*
-eu	*feu*	-eux	*feux*
-ou	*bijou*	-oux	*bijoux*

Note that the rules about making nouns feminine apply only to some nouns that refer to people and animals. They do not apply to objects, which have either a masculine form or a feminine form, never both.

Definite Articles

An article is the part of speech used in front of a noun to indicate the noun's application: whether it is specific, unspecific, or partial. The three kinds of French articles—definite, indefinite, and partitive—must agree in gender and number with the nouns they modify.

The French definite article corresponds to 'the' in English. There are four forms of the French definite article: *le*, *la*, *l'*, and *les*. Which definite article to use depends on three things: the noun's gender, number, and first letter. If the noun is plural, use *les*. If it's singular starting with a vowel or mute h, use *l'*. If it's singular and starts with a consonant or aspirated h, use *le* if it's masculine and *la* if it's feminine.

SINGULAR

MASCULINE	FEMININE	BEFORE VOWEL OR MUTE H
le	*la*	*l'*
le garçon	*la fille*	*l'ami, l'homme*

PLURAL

MASCULINE	FEMININE	BEFORE VOWEL OR MUTE H
les	*les*	*les*
les garçons	*les filles*	*les amis, les hommes*

When learning articles, it is important to know that the letter h is always silent in French, but it comes in two varieties: *h muet* (mute h) and *h aspiré* (aspirated h). The only difference between the two is that a mute h allows contractions and liaisons in front of it, and an aspirated h does not. In other words, a word that begins with a mute h acts as if it begins with a vowel, while one that begins with an aspirated h acts like it begins with a consonant.

The definite article has two main uses:

To indicate a specific noun.

Je vais à la banque.	I'm going to the bank.
Voici le livre que je veux.	Here is the book I want.

To indicate the general sense of a noun.

J'aime les fraises.	I like strawberries.
C'est la vie !	That's life!

Note that the English article is not used when talking about a noun in the general sense.

Indefinite Articles

The singular French indefinite article corresponds to "a," "an," or "one" in English. The plural corresponds to "some." There are three forms of the French indefinite article: *un, une,* and *des.* The plural indefinite article is the same for masculine and feminine nouns, while the singular has forms for masculine and feminine. Unlike the definite article, the indefinite article does not change according to the first letter of the noun.

SINGULAR	MASCULINE	FEMININE
	un	une
	un garçon	une fille
	un ami	une amie

PLURAL	MASCULINE	FEMININE
	des	des
	des garçons	des filles
	des amis	des amies

The indefinite article usually refers to a non-specific person or thing:

J'ai vu un homme.	I saw a man.
Il veut des pommes.	He wants some apples.

The indefinite article can also refer to one of something:

Il y a un étudiant dans la salle.	There is one student in the room.
J'ai acheté seulement une pomme.	I bought only one apple.

Alert!

When referring to a person's profession with state-of-being verbs like *être* (to be) and *devenir* (to become), the indefinite article is not used in French (although it is used in English): *Je suis professeur* (I am a teacher). *Il va devenir médecin* (He's going to become a doctor).

In a negative construction, the indefinite article changes to *de*, meaning "not any":

J'ai des stylos.	I have some pens.
Je n'ai pas de stylos.	I don't have any pens.

Partitive Articles

The French partitive article corresponds to "some" or "any" in English. There are four forms of the French partitive article: *du, de la, de l',* and *des.* Note that, like the definite article, the partitive article has four forms, and the one to use depends on three things: the noun's gender, number, and first letter. If the noun is plural, use *des.* If it's singular starting with a vowel or mute h, use *de l'.* If it's singular and starts with a consonant or aspirated h, use *du* if it's masculine and *de la* if it's feminine.

SINGULAR	MASCULINE	FEMININE	BEFORE VOWEL OR MUTE H
	du	*de la*	*de l'*
	du pain	*de la glace*	*de l'eau*
	du thé	*de la bière*	*de l'huile*

SINGULAR	MASCULINE	FEMININE	BEFORE VOWEL OR MUTE H
	des	*des*	*des*
	des pois	*des asperges*	*des haricots*

The partitive article indicates an unknown or unspecified quantity of something, usually food or drink. It is often omitted in English.

Veux-tu du thé ?	Do you want (some) tea?
J'ai mangé de la salade hier.	I ate (some) salad yesterday.
Nous avons des petits pois.	We have (some) peas.

The partitive is usually used when discussing eating or drinking, because one normally only eats some butter or cheese, for example, not all of it. If you want to say that you ate all of something, use the definite article:

J'ai mangé des frites.	I ate some fries (a handful).
J'ai mangé les frites.	I ate the fries (all of them).
Il va acheter du beurre.	He's going to buy some butter (one pound).
Il va acheter le beurre.	He's going to buy the butter (all they have).

The partitive indicates that the quantity is unknown or uncountable. When the quantity is known/countable and equals one, use the indefinite article.

Je vais acheter du café.	I'm going to buy some coffee (a pound or so).
Je vais acheter un café.	I'm going to buy a coffee (at the coffe shop).
Il a mangé de la tarte.	He ate some pie.
Il a mangé une tarte.	He ate a (whole) pie.

With adverbs of quantity such as *beaucoup de* (a lot), *peu de* (a little), *assez de* (enough), *plus de* (more), and *moins de* (less), *de* is used instead of the partitive article:

Il y a beaucoup de problèmes.	There are a lot of problems.
Il a peu d'énergie.	He has little energy.
As-tu assez d'argent ?	Do you have enough money?
J'ai moins de glace que Thierry.	I have less ice cream than Thierry.

Like the indefinite article, the partitive article changes to *de*, meaning "not any," in a negative construction.

J'ai mangé de la soupe.	I ate some soup.
Je n'ai pas mangé de soupe.	I didn't eat any soup.
Veux-tu du thé ?	Do you want some tea?
Ne veux-tu pas de thé ?	Don't you want any tea?

French articles can be confusing for students of French because they have to agree with the nouns they modify and because they don't always correspond to articles in other languages. As a general rule, ignore articles in your own language and be aware that French nouns are nearly always preceded by an article. The major exceptions are with state-of-being verbs and non-descriptive adjectives (see Chapter 3).

Summary of French Articles

	DEFINITE	INDEFINITE	PARTITIVE
masculine	*le*	*un*	*du*
feminine	*la*	*une*	*de la*
in front of a vowel	*l'*	*un/une*	*de l'*
plural	*les*	*des*	*des*

Exercices de contrôle

A. For each of the masculine nouns listed, provide the feminine form, including the appropriate article.

1. *un étudiant*   _____

2. *l'employé*   _____

3. *un dentiste*   _____

4. *les fonctionnaires*   _____

5. *le cousin*   _____

6. *des amis*   _____

7. *les artistes*   _____

8. *un patron*   _____

9. *l'Américain*   _____

10. *les traducteurs*   _____

B. For each of the singular nouns listed, provide the plural form, including the appropriate article.

a. *un homme*   _____

b. *une femme*   _____

c. *l'ami*   _____

d. *la tarte*   _____

e. *une salade*   _____

f. *l'idée*   _____

g. *un manteau*   _____

h. *le feu*   _____

i. *un gâteau*   _____

j. *la vie*   _____

Chapter 3

Adjectives

THE THIRD PART of speech you need to learn about to master French grammar is the adjective. Adjectives are words that modify (describe) nouns. Adjectives can qualify, specify, or limit the nouns they modify, and can describe shape, color, size, and many other aspects of nouns. Adjectives allow you to be more specific and clear when explaining or describing something in French.

Introduction to Adjectives

Because they are descriptive, adjectives are not a required part of a sentence the way, say, verbs are. Certainly they change the meaning of a sentence (compare "I bought a house" to "I bought an old, yellow house") but the second sentence still makes sense without the adjectives "old" and "yellow." Thus the purpose of adjectives is to make the nouns they modify more specific.

Adjectives are an important part of speech in both English and French, but French adjectives are very different from their English counterparts, for two main reasons. Firstly, in English, adjectives are always found in front of the noun, but most French adjectives are placed after it. Secondly, French adjectives change to agree in gender and number with the nouns that they modify.

There are two categories of adjectives: descriptive and non-descriptive. Descriptive adjectives are those that describe a noun in terms of color, size, beauty, intellect, etc. Everything from "authoritative" to "zany" falls into the category of descriptive adjectives.

 Fact

In grammar classes, you probably heard an adjective defined as a word that describes a noun. While this is accurate, it is also somewhat misleading, as it tends to make one think only of descriptive adjectives. Non-descriptive adjectives can be a more difficult concept, because they modify nouns without describing them.

Non-descriptive adjectives, on the other hand, are those that modify a noun by characterizing, specifying, or limiting it without describing it. There are numerous types of non-descriptive adjectives, each of which having its own particular purpose and usage:

- **Demonstrative adjectives** indicate which specific noun is being talked about (*ce livre*—this book)
- **Exclamative adjectives** express a strong sentiment such as admiration about a noun (*quel livre !*—what a book!)
- **Indefinite adjectives** modify nouns in an unspecific sense (*chaque livre*—each book)
- **Interrogative adjectives** ask for information about a noun (*quel livre ?*—which book?)
- **Negative adjectives** negate a noun (*aucun livre*—no book)
- **Possessive adjectives** indicate the owner of a noun (*mon livre*—my book)

The first four types of non-descriptive adjectives are explained in this chapter, while negative and possessive adjectives are explained in Chapters 12 and 19, respectively.

Making Adjectives Feminine and Plural

Like articles, French adjectives have to agree in gender and number with the nouns that they modify, which means that there can be up to four forms of each adjective: masculine singular, feminine singular, masculine plural, and feminine plural. The rules for making the majority of adjectives feminine and plural are very similar to those for nouns.

Most adjectives add *e* for feminine and *s* for plural:

vert (green)

	SINGULAR	PLURAL
masculine	*vert*	*verts*
feminine	*verte*	*vertes*

grand (big, tall)

	SINGULAR	PLURAL
masculine	*grand*	*grands*
feminine	*grande*	*grandes*

When the masculine adjective ends in e, there is no difference between the masculine and feminine forms:

rouge (red)

	SINGULAR	PLURAL
masculine	*rouge*	*rouges*
feminine	*rouge*	*rouges*

stupide (stupid)

	SINGULAR	PLURAL
masculine	*stupide*	*stupides*
feminine	*stupide*	*stupides*

When the adjective ends in *s* or *x*, there is no difference between the singular and plural masculine forms:

gris (gray)

	SINGULAR	PLURAL
masculine	*gris*	*gris*
feminine	*grise*	*grises*

heureux (happy)

	SINGULAR	PLURAL
masculine	*heureux*	*heureux*
feminine	*heureuse*	*heureuses*

As with nouns, there are some irregular gender patterns.

ENDING	MASCULINE	FEM. ENDING	FEMININE
-c	*blanc*	-che	*blanche*
-el	*actuel*	-elle	*actuelle*
-en	*canadien*	-enne	*canadienne*
-er	*cher*	-ère	*chère*
-et	*complet*	-ète	*complète*
-eur	*flatteur*	-euse	*flatteuse*
-eux	*heureux*	-euse	*heureuse*
-f	*naïf*	-ve	*naïve*
-il	*gentil*	-ille	*gentille*
-on	*bon*	-onne	*bonne*
-s	*bas*	-sse	*basse*
-ul	*nul*	-ulle	*nulle*

There are also some irregular plural patterns.

ENDING	MASCULINE (SINGULAR)	MASCULINE (PLURAL)
-al	*idéal*	*idéaux*
-eau	*beau*	*beaux*

Finally, there are six French adjectives that have irregular feminine forms, as well as a special form used only when they are placed in front of a singular masculine noun that begins with a vowel or a mute *h*.

The Six Adjectives with Irregular Feminine Forms

	SINGULAR			PLURAL	
Adjective	masc	vowel	fem	masc	fem
beautiful	beau	bel	belle	beaux	belles
this	ce	cet	cette	ces	ces
new	nouveau	nouvel	nouvelle	nouveaux	nouvelles
crazy	fou	fol	folle	fous	folles
soft	mou	mol	molle	mous	molles
old	vieux	vieil	vieille	vieux	vieilles

Demonstrative and Indefinite Adjectives

Demonstrative and indefinite adjectives are opposites: demonstrative adjectives are used to indicate a specific noun, while indefinite adjectives modify nouns without being specific.

Demonstrative Adjectives

Demonstrative adjectives are used to indicate a specific noun. The English demonstrative adjectives are: this, that, these, those. As you can see, they agree in number but not gender with the noun they modify. In French, on the other hand, demonstrative adjectives must agree in gender *and* number:

	SINGULAR	PLURAL
masculine	ce / cet	ces
feminine	cette	ces

Note that *ce* becomes *cet* in front of a singular masculine noun that begins with a vowel or mute *h*, and that *ces* is used in front of any plural noun, whether it is singular or plural. "*Cettes*" does not exist.

Ce livre est intéressant.	This (That) book is interesting.
Cet étudiant parle bien.	This (That) student speaks well.
Cet homme est beau.	This (That) man is handsome.
Cette femme ne travaille pas.	This (That) woman doesn't work.
Ces professeurs sont intelligents.	These (Those) teachers are smart.

 Alert!

The adjective *cet* is used only if it immediately precedes a singular masculine noun that begins with a vowel or mute *h*. Therefore, you would say *cet homme*, but *ce jeune homme*.

Depending on context, the singular demonstrative adjectives *ce*, *cet*, and *cette* can all mean "this" or "that," while the plural *ces* can mean "these" or "those." The only way to clearly distinguish between this/that and these/those is with the suffixes *-ci* (here) and *-là* (there).

Ce livre-ci est rouge.	This book is red.
Ce livre-là est vert.	That book is green.
Cet homme-ci est beau.	This man is handsome.
Cette femme-là est belle.	That woman is beautiful.
Ces professeurs-ci sont plus intelligents que ces professeurs-là.	These teachers are more intelligent than those teachers.

Indefinite Adjectives

Indefinite adjectives modify nouns in a way that makes them unspecific. Words like "every," "any," "all," and "each" are examples of indefinite adjectives.

Chaque personne doit essayer.	Each person must try.
Il y a trois autres livres.	There are three other books.
Tous les vêtements sont noirs.	All of the clothes are black.
Il a certaines idées.	He has certain ideas.
Plusieurs étudiants sont absents.	Several students are absent.
Diverses personnes m'ont parlé.	Various people talked to me.

Like other French adjectives, indefinite adjectives need to agree with the nouns they modify in gender and number.

	MASCULINE	FEMININE	MASC PLURAL	FEM PLURAL
other	*autre*	*autre*	*autres*	*autres*
certain	*certain*	*certaine*	*certains*	*certaines*
each	*chaque*	*chaque*		
various			*divers*	*diverses*
many	*maint*	*mainte*	*maints*	*maintes*
several			*plusieurs*	*plusieurs*
some, a few	*quelque*	*quelque*	*quelques*	*quelques*
some, any	*tel*	*telle*	*tels*	*telles*
all	*tout*	*toute*	*tous*	*toutes*

 Essential

Chaque has only a singular form and thus can only be used with singular nouns and the third person singular of the verb: *Chaque membre est ici* (Each member is here). Likewise, *divers* and *plusieurs* have only plural forms, can modify only plural nouns, and must use the third person plural verb: *Plusieurs membres sont ici* (Several members are here).

An indefinite adjective + a noun can be replaced with an indefinite pronoun. You will learn about this in depth in the next chapter.

Interrogative and Exclamative Adjectives

French interrogative and exclamative adjectives are two different types of adjectives with different meanings and uses. However, it makes sense to learn them together because they have identical forms:

	SINGULAR	PLURAL
masculine	*quel*	*quels*
feminine	*quelle*	*quelles*

Interrogative Adjectives

Sometimes French grammar is much more strict than English grammar. A simple question like "What book do you want?" in English is technically incorrect—in proper English, the question should be "Which book do you want?" In reality, the former construction is much more common than the latter. In French, however, you do not have this option: the French equivalent of which, *quel*, must be used whenever there is more than one noun that you are choosing from.

Basically, *quel* is used whenever you want specific information about a noun.

Quel livre cherches-tu ?	What (Which) book are you looking for?
Quelle heure est-il ?	What time is it?
À quelle heure est-il parti ?	What time did he leave?
De quels étudiants est-ce qu'il parle ?	What (Which) students is he talking about?
Quel est le problème ?	What's the problem?
Quelle est la différence ?	What's the difference?
Peux-tu me prêter un livre ?	Could you loan me a book?
Quel livre ?	What (which) book?

Exclamative Adjectives

Exclamative adjectives are placed in front of nouns to express admiration, astonishment, indignation, or another strong sentiment, and are usually translated as "what" or "what a."

Quel bateau !	What a boat!
Quelle catastrophe !	What a catastrophe!
Quelles jolies fleurs !	What pretty flowers!
Quels étudiants intelligents !	What intelligent students!

 Question?

What's the difference between *quel* as an exclamative adjective and *quel* as an interrogative adjective?
An exclamative adjective expresses a strong emotion about the noun it modifies (*Quel livre !*—What a book!), while an interrogative adjective asks a question about the noun (*Quel livre ?*—Which book?)

Position of Adjectives

The position of adjectives can be a problem for learners of French, because the type and meaning of the adjective dictate whether it should be placed before or after the noun. This concept can be frustrating, but with patience and practice it will eventually become second nature.

After the Noun

Descriptive adjectives are usually placed after the noun they modify, particularly when they have an analytical meaning. In other words, they classify the noun into a certain category, such as shape, color, taste, nationality, religion, social class, personality, or mood. In addition, when a present or past participle is used as an adjective, it is always placed after the noun.

l'écriture ronde	round handwriting
a un livre rouge	a red book
du café noir	black coffee
a un homme *français*	a French novel
a une église chrétienne	a Christian church
a une famille bourgeoise	a middle-class family
a un livre intéressant	a interesting book
a un débat passionné	a lively debate

Before the Noun

A small number of adjectives are placed before the noun, and the acronym "BANGS" can help you memorize most of them:

Beauty
Age
Number
Good and bad
Size

These adjectives, as well as a few others, precede the noun because they are considered inherent qualities. Examples of these types of adjectives are below.

une jolie fleur	pretty flower
un jeune enfant	young child
une nouvelle voiture	new car
une bonne idée	good idea
un petit problème	small problem
les sincères condoléances	sincere sympathy
les vagues promesses	vague promises
une gentille fille	kind girl

In addition, all non-descriptive adjectives are placed before the noun.

Important things to note are that when a descriptive adjective precedes a noun, it goes between the article and the noun (*le gentil garçon*) and that when a non-descriptive adjective is used, there is no article (*ce garçon*). If a noun is modified by a descriptive adjective (that precedes the noun according to the above rules) and a non-descriptive adjective, the word order is non-descriptive adjective + descriptive adjective + noun (*ce gentil garçon*).

 Essential

When *grand* refers to height as opposed to size, it follows the noun it modifies, rather than preceding it as you would expect from the BANGS acronym: *un homme grand* (tall man), but *une grande boîte* (large box).

Adjectives that have two meanings may be placed on either side of the verb. When the meaning is figurative, the adjective is placed before the noun, and when the meaning is analytic or literal, the adjective is placed after the noun.

FIGURATIVE MEANING	
mes vertes années	my green (fruitful) years
un grand homme	a great man
un triste garçon	a sad (mean or bad) boy
mon ancien professeur	my old (former) teacher
un certain regard	a certain (type of) look

ANALYTIC/LITERAL MEANING	
des chemises vertes	green shirts
un homme grand	a tall man
un garçon triste	a sad (crying) boy
une victoire certaine	a certain (assured) victory

Exercices de contrôle

A. For each of the singular masculine adjectives listed, provide the singular feminine, plural masculine, and plural feminine forms.

1. *noir*

   _____

2. *grand*

   _____

3. *petit*

   _____

4. *facile*

   _____

5. *gros*

   _____

6. *discret*

   _____

7. *franc*

   _____

8. *jaloux*

   _____

9. *bon*

   _____

10. *tranquille*

    _____

B. Put together the following words, in the correct order, and be sure to change the articles and adjective to agree with the noun in gender and number, if necessary. The articles may or may not be needed—you must decide. You should be able to determine the gender of some of the nouns; for the others, (m) indicates that the noun is masculine and (f) means it's feminine.

a. *joli | fille (f) | le*

b. *vert | robe (f) | un*

c. *heureux | garçon (m) | le*

d. *jeune | cousines | le*

e. *idéal | endroits (m) | un*

f. *bon | amies | le*

g. *ce | livres (m) | le*

h. *quel | intéressant | discussion (f)*

i. *certain | nouveau | étudiantes*

j. *ce | petit | rouge | tables (f)*

Chapter 4

Pronouns

PRONOUNS ARE THE part of speech that allows you to avoid repeating yourself. Instead of saying "I like John. John is an interesting person. What do you think of John?" you can say "I like John. He's an interesting person. What do you think of him?" In other words, pronouns substitute for nouns. They can save you time when speaking French and allow your language to sound more natural.

Introduction to Pronouns

There are many different kinds of pronouns, which are divided into two categories: personal and impersonal. These terms have nothing to do with personality, but rather with grammatical person.

Grammatical person refers to the six possible combinations of "number" and "person" that let you know who or what is performing or receiving the action of a verb. Number is divided into singular (one) and plural (more than one). As for person, you have first person (the speaker), second person (the listener), and third person (neither the speaker nor the listener). So there are two numbers and three persons, making a total of six grammatical persons, each of which has at least one of each type of personal pronoun.

	SINGULAR	PLURAL
1st person	I	we
2nd person	you	you
3rd person	he, she, it, one	they

Personal Pronouns

Personal pronouns change according to the grammatical person that they represent. There are five types of French personal pronouns:

1. Subject
2. Stressed
3. Direct object
4. Indirect object
5. Reflexive

You will learn the differences between subject and stressed pronouns later in this chapter.

Impersonal Pronouns

Impersonal pronouns do not have any relation to grammatical person and therefore do not vary with it. However, some impersonal pronouns change to agree in gender and number with the noun that they replace. There are a number of different types of impersonal pronouns, many of which you will learn more about in later chapters:

- Adverbial pronouns
- Demonstrative pronouns
- Indefinite demonstrative pronouns
- Indefinite pronouns
- Interrogative pronouns
- Negative pronouns
- Possessive pronouns
- Relative pronouns
- Indefinite relative pronouns

Demonstrative, indefinite, and indefinite demonstrative pronouns are explained in this chapter.

Subject Pronouns

Subject pronouns are the most common personal pronoun. They indicate the subject of a verb: who or what is performing its action.

Subject Pronouns

	SINGULAR		PLURAL	
1st person	I	*je*	we	*nous*
2nd person	you	*tu/ vous*	you	*vous*
3rd person	he, it	*il*	they	*ils*
3rd person	she, it	*elle*	they	*elles*
3rd person	one	*on*		

There are several things to take note of in this table. The French first person singular pronoun, *je*, is only capitalized at the beginning of a sentence, unlike its English counterpart "I." *Je* becomes *j'* when followed by a vowel or mute *h*.

Je dois étudier.	I have to study.
Hier, j'ai vu Paul.	Yesterday, I saw Paul.

Another thing to note is that *Il* and *elle* mean "he" and "she," respectively, and both of them can also mean "it." Because all nouns are either masculine or feminine, they can be replaced by the third person subject pronouns which correspond to their gender. Thus *il* can refer to a male (he) or a masculine noun (it) and *elle* can refer to a female (she) or a feminine noun (it):

David arrive à midi. Il arrive à midi.	David is arriving at noon. He's arriving at noon.
Le livre est ici. Il est ici.	The book is here. It's here.
La pomme est rouge. Elle est rouge.	The apple is red. It's red.

On is the indefinite subject pronoun. Its English equivalents can be the passive voice or indefinite subjects like "people," "one," "they," or "you." *On* is also used informally in place of *nous*:

On ne fait pas ça.	That isn't done.
On n'entend pas ça.	You don't hear that.
On est fous !	People are crazy!
On va sortir ce soir.	We're going out tonight.

Ils is used for men, male nouns, and mixed gender groups (in other words, *ils* is the default), while *elles* can be used only for a group of women and/or female nouns—it can be used only when there is not a single male in the group.

Thierry et Luc vont .../	Thierry and Luc are going .../
Ils vont...	They are going ...
Ana et Lise ont .../	Ana and Lise have .../
Elles ont...	They have ...
Thierry et Ana aiment .../	Thierry and Ana like .../
Ils aiment...	They like ...

Note that the pronouns *il, elle,* and *on* are all third person singular personal pronouns and thus take the same verb conjugation: *Il va à l'école, On va à l'école.* Likewise, *ils* and *elles* both take the third person plural conjugation. Perhaps the most important difference between English and French subject pronouns is that French has two words for "you": *tu* and *vous.* In French, two important distinctions are made when referring to "you": Is there one person or more than one? Is it someone to whom you want to indicate closeness (a friend, parent, pet) or someone to whom you wish to show respect or distance (a stranger, a doctor, teacher, lawyer)? Once you've answered these questions, you'll know which "you" to use: *tu* for singular and familiar, and *vous* for formal and/ or plural. These words are not interchangeable, so it is very important to understand when and why to use each of them. Otherwise, you may inadvertently insult someone by using the wrong you.

 **Essential**

Vous is both formal and plural, meaning that whether you are speaking to a single person to whom you wish to show respect or distance, or more than one person (whether or not you want to show respect or distance), you use *vous*. *Tu* is used only when talking to a single person to whom you are close.

Tu is the familiar you. It demonstrates a certain closeness and informality. Use *tu* when speaking to a:

- friend
- peer
- relative
- child
- pet

Vous is the formal and plural you. It is used to show respect or maintain a certain distance or formality with any person. In addition, *vous* is always used when you are talking to more than one person. Use *vous* when speaking to:

- someone you don't know well
- an older person
- an authority figure
- anyone to whom you wish to show respect and/ or distance
- two or more people, animals, etc.

Some people follow the guideline of using whatever the other person uses with them. This can be misleading: someone in authority may use *tu* with you, but that certainly doesn't mean that you can respond in kind. When in doubt, use *vous*. You may sound like a snob if you use *vous* with someone that you should use *tu* with, but that's better than sounding disrespectful by using *tu* with someone you should use *vous* with.

The importance of using the correct "you" cannot be overstressed. There are even verbs that express this concept: *tutoyer* means to call someone *tu* and *vouvoyer* means to call someone *vous*. As a general rule, use *vous* when you're not sure—it's better to show someone too much respect than not enough!

Stressed Pronouns

Stressed pronouns, also known as disjunctive pronouns, are the type of personal pronoun used to emphasize a noun or another pronoun. There are nine forms:

Stressed Pronoun Forms

	SINGULAR		PLURAL	
1st person	me	*moi*	us	*nous*
2nd person	you	*toi*	you	*vous*
3rd person	him	*lui*	them	*eux*
3rd person	her	*elle*	them	*elles*
3rd person	oneself	*soi*		

French stressed pronouns correspond in some ways to their English counterparts, but are very different in other ways. In fact, English translation sometimes requires different sentence structures altogether.

Stressed pronouns are used in the following ways.

1. To emphasize nouns or pronouns.

Je pense qu'il a raison.	*I* think he's right.
Moi, je pense qu'il a tort.	*I* think he's wrong.
Je ne sais pas, moi.	*I* don't know.

This type of emphasis may also follow the expression *c'est.*

C'est toi qui étudies l'art.	*You*'re (the one who is) studying art.
C'est elle qui aime Paris.	*She* loves Paris/ *She* is the one who loves Paris.

For extra emphasis, you can add *-même*:

Prépare-t-il le dîner lui-même ?	Is he making dinner himself?
Nous le ferons nous-mêmes.	We'll do it ourselves.

2. When a sentence has more than one subject, stressed pronouns are used. Note that this is different than English, which uses subject pronouns whether there is one subject or more than one.

Michel et moi jouons au tennis.	Michel and I are playing tennis.
Toi et lui êtes très gentils.	You and he are very kind.

 Essential

When using two subject pronouns, it can be a little tricky to figure out which verb conjugation to use. What you need to do is think about which plural pronoun would replace the two singular ones. For example, *Michel et moi* (Michel and I) would be replaced by *nous* (we), so the verb conjugation would be the *nous* form.

3. In response to questions, the stressed pronoun may be used as it is in English (though whether this usage is correct in English is a matter of some debate).

Qui va à la plage ? Lui.	Who's going to the beach? Him / He is.
C'est moi ou toi qui savais	Is it me or you who knew
la vérité ? Toi.	the truth? You.

4. After prepositions

Vas-tu manger sans moi ?	Are you going to eat without me?
David habite chez elle.	David lives at her house.
Ce stylo est à toi.	This is your pen.

5. After *que* in comparisons (see Chapter 16)

Elle est plus grande que toi.	She is taller than you (are).
Tu es aussi jolie qu'elle.	You are as pretty as she (is).

Like *je*, *que* becomes *qu'* in front of a vowel or mute *h*. *Soi* is used for unspecified persons (when the subject is *on* or another indefinite pronoun):

On doit rester chez soi.	One needs to stay at home.
Chacun pour soi.	Every man for himself.
Il ne faut pas parler de soi.	One shouldn't talk about oneself.

Demonstrative Pronouns

Demonstrative pronouns refer to a previously-mentioned noun in a sentence: this one, that one, the one(s), these, those. They must agree with the gender and number of the noun(s) they are referring to.

Demonstrative Pronouns

	SINGULAR	PLURAL
masculine	*celui*	*ceux*
feminine	*celle*	*celles*

Demonstrative pronouns essentially replace a demonstrative adjective + a noun. Therefore, like demonstrative adjectives, demonstrative pronouns can refer to something nearby or far away. That is, *celui* and *celle* can mean "this one" or "that one," while *ceux* and *celles* can mean "these" or "those."

Demonstrative pronouns must be used in one of three types of constructions:

1. With the suffixes *-ci* or *-là* (see demonstrative adjectives, Chapter 3) in order to distinguish between this one/these and that one/those.

    Quelle fille l'a fait, celle-ci ou celle-là ?
    Which girl did it, this one or that one?

    Je ne sais pas si je veux ceux-ci ou ceux-là.
    I don't know if I want these or those.

2. With a preposition, usually *de*, to indicate possession or origin.

    Quel film veux-tu voir ? Celui de la France ou celui du Canada ?
    Which movie do you want to see? The one from France or (the one from) Canada?

    Je ne peux pas décider entre ces deux robes. Celle de soie est plus jolie mais aussi plus chère que celle de coton.
    I can't decide between these two dresses. The silk one is prettier but also more expensive than the cotton one.

3. With a relative pronoun + dependent clause (see chapter 15).

Celui qui a menti sera puni.
He who / Whoever lied will be punished.

Ceux qui sont polis recevront un cadeau.
Those who are polite will receive a gift.

Indefinite Demonstrative Pronouns

Indefinite (also known as neutral or invariable) demonstrative pronouns do not refer to any particular noun and thus do not have different forms for gender and number. Indefinite demonstrative pronouns can refer to something abstract, like an idea or a situation, or to something indicated but unnamed. There are four indefinite demonstrative pronouns:

ce	this (one), it (+ verb)
ceci	this (+ verb)
cela	that (+ verb)
ça	this, that (+ verb)

Note that there is no distinction made between masculine and feminine.

Ce is used mainly with the verb *être* either in the basic expression *c'est* or in various impersonal expressions. *Ce* and "ceci", "cela" may also be followed by *pouvoir* or *devoir* + *être*.

C'est une bonne décision.	That's a good decision.
C'est difficile à dire.	It's hard to say.
C'est important d'essayer.	It's important to try.
Travailler, c'est essentiel.	Working is essential.
Ce doit être un film intéressant.	This must be an interesting movie.
Ce peut être faux.	It could be false.

Less commonly and more formally, *ce* can be used without a verb, especially in writing:

J'étudie en France, ce en tant qu'auditeur libre.
I study in France (and this) as an auditor.

Pour ce, nous sommes condamnés.
Therefore/For this we are condemned.

Ceci and *cela* are used in place of *ce* when followed by any other verb, although *ceci* is rare in spoken French. Speakers usually use *cela* to mean either "this" or "that." *Ceci* is most commonly used when you want to be sure to distinguish between "this" and "that."

Dites-lui ceci/ cela de ma part.	Tell him this from me.
Qui a fait cela ?	Who did this?
Cela me plaît.	That pleases me.
Qu'est-ce que c'est que cela ?	What is that?
Je veux ceci, pas cela.	I want this, not that.

Ça is an informal contraction of *cela* (and *ceci*) and thus is used when speaking informally (basically, when speaking to someone with whom you use *tu*).

Dis-lui ça de ma part.	Tell him this from me.
Qui a fait ça ?	Who did this?
Ça me plaît.	That pleases me.
Qu'est-ce que c'est que ça ?	What is that?
Je veux ceci (or ça), pas ça.	I want this, not that.

Indefinite Pronouns

French indefinite pronouns, sometimes called affirmative indefinite pronouns, are nonspecific. They can be the subject of a sentence, the object of a verb, or the object of a preposition.

Tout le monde est prêt.	Everyone is ready.
Je veux te montrer quelque chose.	I want to show you something.
J'ai des idées pour chacun.	I have ideas for each one.

The French indefinite pronouns are:

un(e) autre	another one
d'autres	others
certain(e)s	certain ones
chacun(e)	each one
on	one
plusieurs	several
quelque chose	something
quelqu'un	someone
quelques-uns	some, a few
soi	oneself
tel	one, someone
tout	everything
tout le monde	everyone

The pronouns *un autre*, *d'autres*, *certain*, *chacun*, *plusieurs*, and *quelques-uns* must have an antecedent (a previously mentioned noun that the pronoun refers back to).

Ton livre est bon, vas-tu en écrire un autre ?
Your book is good, are you going to write another one?

Les étudiants parlent trop . . . je dois punir chacun d'eux.
The students talk too much . . . I have to punish each one (of them).

The pronouns *chacun*, *plusieurs*, and *quelques-uns* can be modified with *d'entre* + *eux*, *elles*, *nous*, or *vous*, or with *de* + noun.

Chacun d'entre nous doit essayer.	Each of us has to try.
Quelques-uns d'entre eux réussiront.	Some of them will succeed.
Plusieurs de vos idées sont bonnes.	Several of your ideas are good.

The pronouns *chacun*, *quelque chose*, *quelqu'un*, *tout*, and *tout le monde* always take the third person singular form of the verb.

J'espère que tout va bien	I hope everything is ok.
Tout le monde l'a essayé.	Everyone tried it.

When *quelque chose* and *quelqu'un* are followed by a modifier (like an adjective), the preposition *de* must be used between the pronoun and the modifier.

J'ai vu quelqu'un de bizarre.	I saw someone strange.
Elle cherche quelque chose de bien.	She's looking for something good.

Exercices de contrôle

A. For each of the following, provide the French subject and stressed pronoun.

1. I _____

2. you (singular) _____

3. he _____

4. she _____

5. one _____

6. we _____

7. you (plural) _____

8. they (masculine) _____

9. they (feminine) _____

10. it _____

B. Translate the following words into French, and state which kind of pronoun they are. Some of these may have more than one correct response.

a. this one (masculine) _____

b. these (feminine) _____

c. that one (masculine) _____

d. this _____

e. that _____

f. another one _____

g. each one _____

h. several _____

i. something _____

j. everyone _____

Chapter 5

Introduction to Verbs

THE VERB IS THE ACTION WORD in a sentence—the word that says what happens (I *walk*) or describes a state of being (I *am* happy). Verbs are one of the most essential parts of speech, since they are a required element in every sentence. Nouns, pronouns, adjectives, etc. may not show up in every sentence you use, but verbs will. For example, the shortest grammatically correct sentence in English is "Go!"—that single word in the imperative is a complete sentence.

Conjugating French Verbs

The basic form of a verb is called the infinitive and is considered the name of the verb. The English infinitive is "to" followed by a verb, while the French infinitive is a single word with one of three endings: *-er, -ir,* or *-re.* For example, *parler* (to speak), *finir* (to finish), *vendre* (to sell). When you learn a new French verb, you should make sure to learn its infinitive, since this is the simplest form of the verb and is used as the basis for just about everything you do with it.

All French verbs have to be "conjugated" or "inflected"; that is, changed according to how they are used. In the English present tense, we only have a separate conjugation for the third person singular of a verb: "I want" becomes "he wants." The verb "to be" is the most complicated English verb, with three conjugations: I am, you are, he is. In other tenses and moods, English has a single form: I sang, you sang, I will go, you will go. Again, "to be" is an exception, with two past tense conjugations: I was, you were.

In stark contrast, each French verb has up to six different conjugations in each tense and mood. In most cases, French verbs are conjugated by removing the infinitive ending to find the "radical" or "stem" and then adding the ending appropriate to the grammatical person, tense, and mood. These endings are different for each tense and mood, which means that each verb has dozens of different forms. But don't get discouraged! There are patterns to the conjugations of most verbs. There are a total of five elements in conjugation: number, person, tense, mood, and voice.

Tense, Mood, and Voice

You already learned about number and person with subject pronouns in Chapter 4, so the other three verb conjugation elements you need to understand are tense, mood, and voice. These three work together to explain when an action takes place, the attitude of the speaker toward the action, and the relationship between the subject and verb.

Making Sense of Tense

Tense refers to the time a verb's action takes place. The main tenses are present, past, and future, though there may be two or more verb tenses within those primary categories. For example, there are several French past tenses: simple past (preterite), compound past, imperfect, past perfect, and past anterior.

 Essential

Note that simple and compound tenses don't always match up in French and English. For example, *étudiera* is a simple tense in French, while its translation "will study" is a compound tense in English.

There are two kinds of tenses. A simple tense is a verb form which consists of a single word: *je mange* (I eat), *nous parlons* (we talk), *il étudiera* (he will study). A compound tense is a verb form made up of two words—an auxiliary verb plus past participle: *j'ai mangé* (I have eaten), *il aurait étudié* (he would have studied).

Get in the Mood

Mood refers to the attitude of the speaker toward the action/ state of the verb—how likely or factual a statement is. The French language has three to six moods, depending on how you look at it. The three moods that everyone agrees on are indicative, subjunctive, and imperative, while the conditional, infinitive, and participle may or may not be considered moods by different grammarians.

Indicative

The indicative is what you might call the "normal" mood—it indicates a fact: *J'aime lire* (I like to read), *Nous avons mangé* (We ate). The indicative is the most common mood and has the most tenses.

Subjunctive

The subjunctive expresses subjectivity, such as doubt and unlikelihood: *Je veux que tu le fasses* (I want you to do it), *Il est rare que Chantal sache la réponse* (It's rare for Chantal to know the answer). Note that the subjunctive is rare in English but common in French. It has present and past forms, but no future—the present tense is used for current as well as future actions.

Imperative

The imperative gives a command: *Écris la lettre* (Write the letter), *Allons-y !* (Let's go!) The imperative is the only verb form that does not require a subject or subject pronoun—the conjugation of the verb lets you know who is expected to perform the action of the verb.

Conditional

The conditional describes a condition or possibility: *J'aimerais aider* (I would like to help), *Si tu venais avec nous, tu apprendrais beaucoup* (If you came with us, you would learn a lot). The conditional is considered a separate mood by most but a subcategory of the indicative by a few grammarians.

Infinitive

The infinitive is the name of the verb: *parler* (to speak), *finir* (to finish), *vendre* (to sell). The infinitive is used most commonly after another verb or as a noun; however, as the latter it is usually translated by a gerund (the -ing form of a verb in English): *je veux aller* (I want to go), *voir c'est croire* (seeing is believing).

Fact

The indicative, subjunctive, imperative, and conditional are known as "personal moods," because they are conjugated according to the grammatical person performing the action. The infinitive and participles are not conjugated and are thus called "impersonal moods."

Participle

The participle is the adjectival form of the verb, and comes in two varieties. The present participle ends in *-ant* and is used mainly as a qualifier adjective: *parlant* (speaking), *finissant* (finishing). The past participle usually ends in *-é*, *-i*, or *-u* (for -er, -ir, and -re verbs, respectively) and is used mainly in compound tenses: *parlé* (spoke, spoken), *fini* (finished), *vendu* (sold).

Find Your Voice

Voice refers to the relationship between the subject and verb. There are three voices in French:

1. **Active voice**—the subject performs the action: *Je lave la voiture* (I'm washing the car).
2. **Passive voice**—the action is performed on the subject by an agent, which may be stated or implied: *La voiture est lavée* (The car is being washed), *Le livre a été vendu par Chantal* (The book was sold by Chantal).
3. **Reflexive voice**—the subject performs the action on itself: *Je me lave* (I'm washing myself).

Active voice is the most common voice in French, followed by reflexive voice, which is much more common in French than in English. More than in English, the passive voice is usually avoided in French.

Verb Forms

Once you know the tense and mood that you would like to use, you have a verb form and you can start figuring out its conjugations. There are more than twenty French verb forms, the most important of which are explained in upcoming chapters. To get an idea about how tense and mood fit together in French, take a look at this list:

INDICATIVE

Past:	Preterite, Imperfect, Present perfect, Pluperfect, Past anterior
Present:	Present indicative
Future:	Future indicative, Future perfect

SUBJUNCTIVE

Past:	Past subjunctive, Imperfect subjunctive, Pluperfect subjunctive
Present/Future:	Subjunctive

IMPERATIVE

Past:	Past imperative
Present:	Imperative

CONDITIONAL

Past:	Past conditional
Present/Future:	Conditional

PARTICIPLE

Past:	Past participle
Present:	Present participle

INFINITIVE

Present:	Infinitive
Past:	Past infinitive

Types of Verbs

There are four main types of French verbs: regular, stem-changing, irregular, and reflexive. Another way to divide up verbs is by their endings—all French verbs end in *-er*, *-ir*, or *-re*. For regular verbs, these endings are very important as they indicate which set of verb endings to use when conjugating those verbs. Most French verbs are regular, which means that once you know how to conjugate one regular *-er*, *-ir*, and *-re* verb, you can conjugate the majority of French verbs.

-ER Verbs

This is the largest category of regular French verbs:

aimer	to like or to love
arriver	to arrive or to happen
chanter	to sing
chercher	to look for
danser	to dance
demander	to ask for
détester	to hate
donner	to give
écouter	to listen to
étudier	to study
jouer	to play
parler	to talk or to speak
penser	to think
regarder	to watch or to look at
rêver	to dream
skier	to ski
travailler	to work
trouver	to find
visiter	to visit (a place)

-IR Verbs

The second largest category of regular French verbs is the group of –ir verbs. Following are some of the most useful to know.

abolir	to abolish
agir	to act
avertir	to warn
bâtir	to build
bénir	to bless
choisir	to choose
établir	to establish
étourdir	to stun, deafen, make dizzy
finir	to finish
grossir	to get fat
guérir	to cure, heal, recover
maigrir	to lose weight or to get thin
nourrir	to feed or to nourish
obéir	to obey
punir	to punish
réfléchir	to reflect or to think
remplir	to fill
réussir	to succeed
rougir	to blush or to turn red
vieillir	to grow old

-RE Verbs

The –re verbs compose the smallest category of regular verbs in French. Examples are:

attendre	to wait (for)
défendre	to defend
descendre	to descend
entendre	to hear
perdre	to lose
prétendre	to claim
rendre	to give back or to return something
répondre	to answer
vendre	to sell

Alert!

Although all verbs end in *-er, -ir,* or *-re,* not all verbs are regular. As you study French, you will learn to distinguish between regular and irregular verbs.

Pronominal Verbs

Like all verbs, pronominal verbs have one of the three French verb endings, but they have an additional characteristic: they must be preceded by a reflexive pronoun which indicates that the subject is performing the action of the verb upon itself (*je me lave*—I'm washing myself) or that multiple subjects are performing a reciprocal action (*ils s'écrivent*—they are writing to each other).

Essential

Remember that the verb form that ends in *-er, -ir,* or *-re* is called the infinitive, whereas in English, the infinitive is the verb preceded by the word "to." *-er, -ir,* and *-re* are known as "infinitive endings." The verb without the infinitive ending is called the "stem" or "radical."

Pronominal verbs are what you use for the reflexive voice, and they often have to do with parts of the body or clothing. You can recognize reflexive verbs by the *se* which precedes the infinitive. Here are some common reflexive verbs:

s'asseoir	to sit down
se brosser (les cheveux, les dents)	to brush (one's hair, one's teeth)
se casser (la jambe)	to break (one's leg)
se coiffer	to fix one's hair
se coucher	to go to bed

se déshabiller	to get undressed
se doucher	to take a shower
se fâcher	to get angry
s'habiller	to get dressed
se laver (les mains, la figure)	to wash (one's hands, one's face)
se lever	to get up
se maquiller	to put on makeup
se raser	to shave
se regarder	to look at oneself
se réveiller	to wake up
se souvenir de	to remember

Note in the above list that se becomes s' when followed by a vowel or mute h.

Exercices de contrôle

A. Answer the following questions.

1. What do the following terms mean? Conjugation, infinitive ending, radical

   _____

   _____

2. What are the five conjugation elements?

   _____

3. What are the three infinitive endings?

   _____

4. What are the three main verb tenses?

   _____

5. What's the difference between simple and compound tenses?

   _____

6. What are the six moods?

   _____

7. What's the difference between personal and impersonal moods?

   _____

8. What are the three voices?

   _____

9. What is the biggest category of regular verbs?

   _____

10. What is a pronominal verb and how can you recognize it?

    _____

B. Decide whether each of the following verb forms is an infinitive, present participle, or past participle. If it's a participle, provide the infinitive.

    a. *commencer*   _____

    b. *rendu*   _____

    c. *abolissant*   _____

    d. *établir*   _____

    e. *vendre*   _____

    f. *chantant*   _____

    g. *choisi*   _____

    h. *entendu*   _____

    i. *pensant*   _____

    j. *répondre*   _____

Chapter 6

Present Tense

THE PRESENT TENSE (*le présent*) is the most common French tense. This chapter offers explanations of the conjugations of regular, stem-changing, irregular, and pronominal verbs. This may seem over-whelming at first, but with practice, verb conjugations will become second nature to you. If you're having trouble, just learn one set of conjugations and practice writing them out for a few verbs every day, until you feel comfortable with them. Learn another set and write those out. Eventually, you won't even have to think about conjugations.

Using the Present Tense

The French present tense is used in much the same way as the English present tense, with one major exception. In English, we have what is called "aspect," a grammatical term which indicates the relationship of the verb's action to the passage of time. The three aspects can be seen in these examples: "I eat," "I am eating," and "I do eat." French, however, does not have aspect—all of the above are translated by *je mange*.

If you want to emphasize the fact that something is happening right now as you might with "I am eating," you can use *être en train de*: *Je suis en train de manger*—I am (in the process of) eating (right now).

Regular Verbs

Regular verbs are those that follow one of three sets of conjugation rules. The majority of French verbs are regular, but they are divided into three categories: regular -er verbs, regular -ir verbs, and regular -re verbs, each of which has its own set of conjugations.

-ER Verbs

There are more *-er* verbs than any other type—they are among the most common and useful French verbs. To conjugate an *-er* verb in the present tense, remove the infinitive ending to find the radical and then add the appropriate -er endings, as follows:

je	*-e*	*nous*	*-ons*
tu	*-es*	*vous*	*-ez*
il / elle	*-e*	*ils / elles*	*-ent*

Thus to conjugate *parler* (to talk, speak), you would remove the infinitive ending to find the radical *parl-* and then add the above endings:

je	*parle*	*nous*	*parlons*
tu	*parles*	*vous*	*parlez*
il / elle	*parle*	*ils / elles*	*parlent*

Fact

The *-ent* ending for *ils / elles* is silent, as is the *s* in the *tu* and *nous* forms. All singular forms of -er verbs and the third person plural form are pronounced identically.

Regular verbs that end in *-ier*, like *étudier* (to study), follow the same pattern: drop -er to find the stem *étudi-* and then add the endings. Just be careful to keep the *i*:

j'	étudie	nous	étudions
tu	étudies	vous	étudiez
il / elle	étudie	ils / elles	étudient

Remember that if the verb begins with a vowel or mute h, *je* changes to *j'*.

-IR Verbs

Regular *-ir* verbs are the second largest category of French verbs. To conjugate an *-ir* verb, remove the infinitive ending and then add the *-ir* endings, as follows:

je	-is	nous	-issons
tu	-is	vous	-issez
il / elle	-it	ils / elles	-issent

So to conjugate *choisir* (to choose) you would remove the infinitive ending to find the radical *chois-* and then add the appropriate endings:

je	choisis	nous	choisissons
tu	choisis	vous	choisissez
il / elle	choisit	ils / elles	choisissent

-RE Verbs

The smallest category of regular verbs end in *-re*. To conjugate an *-re* verb, remove the infinitive ending and then add the *-re* endings, as follows:

je	-s	nous	-ons
tu	-s	vous	-ez
il / elle	–	ils / elles	-ent

Thus to conjugate *descendre* (to go down, descend) you would remove the infinitive ending to find the radical *descend-* and then add the appropriate endings:

je	descends	nous	descendons
tu	descends	vous	descendez
il / elle	descend	ils / elles	descendent

Summary of present tense endings for regular verbs

-ER VERBS		-IR VERBS		-RE VERBS	
-e	-ons	-is	-issons	-s	-ons
-es	-ez	-is	-issez	-s	-ez
-e	-ent	-it	-issent	-	-ent

 **Alert!**

All verbs end in *-er, -ir,* or *-re,* but that does not mean that all verbs are conjugated using the same formula. Irreguar verbs don't follow these rules!

Stem-Changing Verbs

There are many French -er verbs that take regular endings but have two different stems. These are called stem-changing verbs, because the stem undergoes spelling changes in certain conjugations. These verbs are classified by their endings—there are seven different types of stem-changing verbs.

-YER Verbs

Verbs that end in *-yer,* such as *payer* (to pay) and *nettoyer* (to clean) change y to i in all forms but *nous* and *vous.* However, this stem change is optional—both of the following sets of conjugations are correct.

STEM CHANGE

je	paie	nous	payons
tu	paies	vous	payez
il / elle	paie	ils / elles	paient

REGULAR

je	paye	nous	payons
tu	payes	vous	payez
il / elle	paye	ils / elles	payent

All -*ayer* verbs follow either of the above conjugation patterns. Some of the most commonly used –*ayer* verbs are:

balayer	to sweep
effrayer	to frighten
essayer	to try
payer	to pay

Verbs that end in -*oyer* or -*uyer* have the stem change, meaning the *y* changes to *i* in all forms but *nous* and *vous*—but for these verbs it is required you conjugate them this way. An example is the conjugation of the verb *nettoyer*:

je	nettoie	nous	nettoyons
tu	nettoies	vous	nettoyez
il / elle	nettoie	ils / elles	nettoient

 Essential

The conjugations for all -*yer* verbs are very similar; the only difference is that the stem change is optional for -*ayer* verbs but required for -*oyer* and -*uyer* verbs.

All -*oyer* and -*uyer* verbs follow the above conjugation pattern. Some examples of –*oyer* and –*uyer* verbs are:

broyer	to grind
employer	to employ
ennuyer	to bore
essuyer	to wipe
nettoyer	to clean
se noyer	to drown
tutoyer	to use "tu"
vouvoyer	to use "vous"

-ELER Verbs

Verbs that end in -*eler*, like *appeler* (to call) double the *l* in all present tense conjugations except with *nous* and *vous*:

j'	*appelle*	*nous*	*appelons*
tu	*appelles*	*vous*	*appelez*
il / elle	*appelle*	*ils / elles*	*appellent*

Most -*eler* verbs follow this conjugation pattern. Some –*eler* verbs are:

appeler	to call
épeler	to spell
rappeler	to call back, recall
renouveler	to renew

The verbs *geler* and *peler* do not follow the typical conjugation pattern for –*eler* verbs, but instead are conjugated like –*eter* verbs, below.

-ETER Verbs

Verbs that end in -*eter* are very similar to the -*eler* verbs: they require you to double the *t* in the stem-changing conjugations in all forms but *nous* and *vous*:

je	jette	nous	jetons
tu	jettes	vous	jetez
il / elle	jette	ils / elles	jettent

Most *-eter* verbs follow this conjugation pattern:

feuilleter	to leaf through
hoqueter	to hiccup
jeter	to throw
projeter	to project
rejeter	to reject

The main exception is *acheter*, which is conjugated like -e_er verbs, below.

-E_ER Verbs

Verbs that end in *-e_er* (where _ indicates any letter, with the exception of most -eler and -eter verbs) have the following stem change: the *e* in the penultimate syllable changes to *è* in all forms but *nous* and *vous*:

je	lève	nous	levons
tu	lèves	vous	levez
il / elle	lève	ils / elles	lèvent

The following verbs require this conjugation pattern:

acheter	to buy
amener	to bring (along)
emmener	to take
enlever	to remove
geler	to freeze
lever	to lift or to raise
mener	to take
peler	to peel
peser	to weigh
promener	to walk

-É_ER Verbs

Verbs that have *é* in the second to last (penultimate) syllable stem change *é* to *è* in all forms except *nous* and *vous*:

je	*considère*	*nous*	*considérons*
tu	*considères*	*vous*	*considérez*
il / elle	*considère*	*ils / elles*	*considèrent*

Below are verbs that follow this stem-change pattern:

céder	*to give up or to dispose of*	*célébrer*	*to celebrate*
compléter	*to complete*	*considérer*	*to consider*
différer	*to differ*	*espérer*	*to hope*
exagérer	*to exaggerate*	*gérer*	*to manage*
inquiéter	*to worry*	*modérer*	*to moderate*
pénétrer	*to enter*	*posséder*	*to possess*
préférer	*to prefer*	*protéger*	*to protect*
refléter	*to reflect*	*répéter*	*to repeat*
révéler	*to reveal*	*suggérer*	*to suggest*

Don't let the verbs containing two letters like *préférer* confuse you! Only the second é (the one in the penultimate syllable) changes.

 Fact

The five categories of stem-changing verbs are known as "boot" or "shoe" verbs, because the stem changes occur in all the singular forms as well as the third person plural, and if you circle the irregular forms with one continuous line, it looks like a boot.

-CER Verbs

Verbs that end in *-cer* have one small spelling change in the *nous* form. Because *c* followed by *o* would make a hard *c* sound (as in the word "cold"), the *c* has to change to *ç* in the *nous* present tense to keep the *c* soft (as in "cell").

je	lance	nous	lançons
tu	lances	vous	lancez
il / elle	lance	ils / elles	lancent

All *-cer* verbs follow this conjugation pattern:

annoncer	to announce	avancer	to advance
commencer	to begin	dénoncer	to denounce
divorcer	to divorce	effacer	to erase
lancer	to throw	menacer	to threaten
placer	to put	prononcer	to pronounce
remplacer	to replace	tracer	to draw

-GER Verbs

There is one small spelling change in the *nous* form of *-ger* verbs. Because *g* followed by *o* would make a hard *g* sound (like in gold), *e* has to be added after the *g* in the *nous* present tense to keep the *g* soft (like in gel).

je	mange	nous	mangeons
tu	manges	vous	mangez
il / elle	mange	ils / elles	mangent

All verbs that end in *-ger* follow this conjugation pattern:

aménager	to fit	arranger	to arrange
bouger	to move	changer	to change
corriger	to correct	décourager	to discourage
dégager	to free	déménager	to move
déranger	to disturb	diriger	to direct
encourager	to encourage	engager	to bind
exiger	to demand	juger	to judge

loger	to lodge	*manger*	to eat
mélanger	to mix	*nager*	to swim
obliger	to oblige	*partager*	to share
plonger	to dive	*ranger*	to tidy (up)
rédiger	to write	*voyager*	to travel

The above is an explanation of present tense conjugations for stem-changing verbs. The stem-changing patterns vary according to verb tense and mood. In the verb conjugation tables at the end of this book, each of the above sample verbs has been conjugated into all the simple tenses, so you can see how the stem changes vary in each tense and mood.

Irregular Verbs

Irregular verbs are those which have conjugations specific to just one or a handful of verbs. The most common irregular verbs are explained in the next chapter, but here are a few groups of irregular verbs that share conjugations.

Irregular -IR Verbs

There are two groups of irregular -ir verbs. The first group includes the verbs *dormir, mentir, partir, sentir, servir, sortir,* and their derivations (e.g., *repartir, endormir*). All of these verbs take the following endings:

SINGULAR		PLURAL	
je	-s	*nous*	-ons
tu	-s	*vous*	-ez
il / elle	-t	*ils / elles*	-ent

These verbs drop the last letter of the radical in the singular forms before adding the above endings, so *dormir* (to sleep) would be conjugated like this:

je	dors	nous	dormons
tu	dors	vous	dormez
il / elle	dort	ils / elles	dorment

The second group of irregular -ir verbs includes *couvrir, cueillir, offrir, ouvrir, souffrir,* and their derivations. The interesting thing about these verbs is that they end in *-ir* but are conjugated exactly like regular *-er* verbs, so the endings are:

je	-e	nous	-ons
tu	-es	vous	-ez
il / elle	-e	ils / elles	-ent

To conjugate *ouvrir* (to open), remove the infinitive ending to find the radical *ouvr-* and then add the appropriate endings:

j'	ouvre	nous	ouvrons
tu	ouvres	vous	ouvrez
il / elle	ouvre	ils / elles	ouvrent

Irregular -RE Verbs

There are three types of irregular -re verbs; the first group includes *rompre* (to break) and its derivatives. The endings for these verbs are as follows:

je	-s	nous	-ons
tu	-s	vous	-ez
il / elle	-t	ils / elles	-ent

These verbs are conjugated just like regular -re verbs with the single exception of the third person singular present tense, which adds a *t* after the stem.

je	romps	nous	rompons
tu	romps	vous	rompez
il / elle	rompt	ils / elles	rompent

The second group of irregular -re verbs includes *prendre* and all of its derivatives. The endings for these verbs are the same as for regular -re verbs:

je	-s	nous	-ons
tu	-s	vous	-ez
il / elle	-	ils / elles	-ent

These verbs drop the *d* in the radical all of the plural forms, and double the *n* in the third person plural.

je	prends	nous	prenons
tu	prends	vous	prenez
il / elle	prend	ils / elles	prennent

The third group of irregular *-re* verbs includes *battre*, *mettre*, and all of their derivatives. The endings for these verbs are again the same as for regular -re verbs; however, these verbs drop the second *t* in the stem of the singular forms.

je	bats	nous	battons
tu	bats	vous	battez
il / elle	bat	ils / elles	battent

Reflexive Verbs

Reflexive verbs are organized according to their regular/irregular/ stem-changing verb classification, but have an additional characteristic: they are preceded by a reflexive pronoun which indicates that the subject is performing the action of the verb upon itself (*je me lave*—I'm washing myself) or that multiple subjects are performing a reciprocal action (*ils s'écrivent*—they are writing to each other). Many verbs have both reflexive and non-reflexive uses. For example, *écrire* means "to write" (a letter, a book, etc.), whereas *s'écrire* means "to write to each other."

Reflexive verbs must be conjugated according to their infinitive ending and regular/stem-changing/irregular status, and also preceded by the appropriate reflexive pronoun. For example:

se laver (to wash oneself)

je	me lave	nous	nous lavons
tu	te laves	vous	vous lavez
il / elle	se lave	ils / elles	se lavent

Reflexive pronouns are a type of personal pronoun used only with pronominal verbs (in the reflexive voice). Pronominal verbs are those which indicate that the subject is performing the action of the verb upon him/her/itself. Reflexive pronouns change to agree with the subject of the sentence. The reflexive pronoun is placed directly in front of the verb in all tenses except the imperative.

The reflexive pronouns are:

je	me / m'	nous	nous
tu	te / t'	vous	vous
il, elle, on	se / s'	ils, elles	se / s'

Me, te, and *se* change to *m', t',* and *s'* in front of a vowel or mute h.

Here are some examples of conjugated reflexive verbs with reflexive pronouns:

Je me lève.	I'm getting up.
Il se rase.	He is shaving.
Nous nous parlons.	We're talking to each other.
Ils ne s'habillent pas.	They aren't getting dressed.

Exercices de contrôle

Conjugate the following verbs into the six present tense forms.

1. *chanter*

_____

2. *aimer*

_____

3. *choisir*

_____

4. *finir*

_____

5. *vendre*

_____

6. *essayer*

_____

7. *commencer*

_____

8. *se casser*

   _____

9. *mettre*

   _____

10. *comprendre*

   _____

Chapter 7

Irregular Verbs

THE CONJUGATIONS YOU LEARNED in the previous chapter allow you to conjugate hundreds of regular verbs. However, French also has a number of irregular verbs, some of which are the most common verbs in the French language. In this chapter, you'll learn how to conjugate and use ten of the most useful irregular French verbs.

Aller—To Go

The French verb *aller* means "to go," and can be used to express most of the English actions associated with "to go".

Je vais à Paris.	I'm going to Paris.
Il va avec vous.	He's going with you.
Je vais au marché.	I'm going to the market.
Vas-tu au cinéma ?	Are you going to the movies?
Ça va bien.	It's going well.

As in English, the verb *aller* can be used to express the near future, usually translated as "going to." The near future is formed with the present tense conjugation of *aller* followed by the infinitive of the action that is about to occur.

Je vais étudier.	I'm going to study.
Ils vont manger dans cinq minutes.	They are going to eat in five minutes.

Aller is also used in some idiomatic expressions:

Je vais à pied.	I'm going on foot.
Ça va sans dire.	That goes without saying.
On y va ?	Shall we go?
Allez-y !	Go ahead!
Allons-y !	Let's go!

Present tense conjugations of *aller*:

je	vais	nous	allons
tu	vas	vous	allez
il / elle	va	ils / elles	vont

See "Appendix A—Verb Tables" for all of the simple tense conjugations for each verb in this chapter.

Avoir—To Have

Avoir means "to have" in most of the same ways that this verb is used in English, including having in one's possession and currently experiencing.

J'ai un crayon.	I have a pencil.
J'ai deux soeurs.	I have two sisters.
J'ai mal à l'estomac.	I have a stomach ache.
J'ai une question.	I have a question.
J'ai été eu.	I've been had (tricked).

Avoir is also used in many idiomatic expressions which are translated by the English verb "to be":

avoir ____ ans	to be ____ years old
avoir chaud	to be hot
avoir de la chance	to be lucky

avoir faim	to be hungry
avoir froid	to be cold
avoir honte	to be ashamed
avoir peur	to be afraid
avoir raison	to be right
avoir soif	to be thirsty
avoir sommeil	to be sleepy
avoir tort	to be wrong

Avoir is the auxiliary for most French verbs in the compound tenses. Here are a few examples:

J'ai déjà mangé.	I have already eaten.
J'aurai fini avant midi.	I will have finished before noon.
Si je t'avais vu, je t'aurais dit bonjour.	If I had seen you, I would have said hello.

Conjugations for *avoir*:

j'	ai	nous	avons
tu	as	vous	avez
il / elle	a	ils / elles	ont

Devoir—Should, Must, To have to

The French verb *devoir* has a number of different meanings related to concepts like obligation, probability, expectation, and inevitability.

Dois-tu étudier ce soir ?	Do you have to study tonight?
Elles doivent partir.	They must / need to leave.
Il doit rentrer avant midi.	He should / will probably be back before noon.
Nous devons travailler plus.	We should work more.
Elle doit être à l'école.	She must be at school.
Il devait perdre un jour.	He had to / was bound to lose one day.

Essential

When you need to say "must" rather than "should," add a word like *absolument* or *vraiment*, as in *Je dois absolument étudier* (I really have to study) and *Il doit vraiment nous aider* (He must help us).

When used transitively (that is, when not followed by a verb), *devoir* means "to owe":

Combien est-ce que je te dois ?   How much do I owe you?
Tu me dois 50 euros.   You owe me 50 euros.

Conjugations for *devoir*:

je	dois	nous	devons
tu	dois	vous	devez
il / elle	doit	ils / elles	doivent

Être—To Be

Être means "to be" in many senses that this verb is used in English. It is used with adjectives, nouns, and adverbs to describe a temporary or permanent state of being:

Il est intelligent.   He is smart.
Je suis à Rome.   I'm in Rome.
Nous sommes américains.   We're American.
Il est ici.   He's here.

When *être* is used to describe someone's profession, the indefinite article is not used:

Mon père est professeur.   My father is a teacher.
Ma mère est avocate.   My mother is a lawyer.
Je suis étudiant.   I'm a student.

 Alert!

Watch out for the English "to be" expressions, which are translated in French by *avoir*, and weather expressions which are translated in French by *faire*.

Être is the auxiliary for some verbs in the compound tenses:

Je suis allé en France.   I went to France.
Il était déjà sorti.   He had already left.
Je serais tombé si . . .   I would have fallen if . . .

Être is also used to form the passive voice:

Les vêtement sont lavés.   The clothes are washed.
Elle est respectée de ses étudiants.   She is respected by her students.

Conjugations of *être*:

je	*suis*	*nous*	*sommes*
tu	*es*	*vous*	*êtes*
il / elle	*est*	*ils / elles*	*sont*

Faire—To Do, Make

Faire literally means "to do" or "to make" in most senses that these verbs are used in English.

Je fais la vaisselle.	I'm doing the dishes.
Je fais mes devoirs.	I'm doing my homework.
Je fais de mon mieux.	I'm doing my best.
Je fais le lit.	I'm making the bed.
Je fais des projets.	I'm making plans.

 Essential

When "to make" is followed by an adjective, it is translated by *rendre*: That makes me sad—*Cela me rend triste.* Also, "to make a decision" is not translated by *faire une décision*, but rather *prendre une décision*: *J'ai pris une décision* (I made a decision).

Faire is also used in numerous idiomatic expressions, most notably those related to weather, sports, and math.

Quel temps fait-il ?	How's the weather?
Il fait frais.	It's chilly.
Je fais du cheval.	I horse-back ride.
Je fais du golf.	I golf.
Un et un font deux.	One plus one equals (makes) two.
Je fais de l'auto-stop.	I'm hitchhiking.
Il fait des économies.	He is saving up.
Ça fait parti de notre projet.	That's part of our plan.

Faire followed by an infinitive is the causative construction, which is used to describe when someone/something has something done, makes someone do something, or causes something to happen.

Je fais réparer la voiture.		I'm having the car repaired.		
Il me fait laver la voiture.		He's making me wash the car.		
Ana fait rougir les garçons.		Ana makes the boys blush.		

Faire conjugations:

je	fais	nous	faisons
tu	fais	vous	faites
il / elle	fait	ils / elles	font

Pouvoir—Can, To Be Able to

The French verb *pouvoir* has a number of different meanings, depending mainly on the tense and mood it is conjugated into. In general, *pouvoir* means "to be able to," and is usually translated by "can," "could," or "may."

Il peut nous aider.	He can help us.
Puis-je m'asseoir ici ?	May I sit here?
Tu pourrais essayer.	You could try.

Pouvoir can express possibility:

Elle peut être partie.	She might/may be gone.
Tu peux le casser.	You might break it.

Pouvoir is often used in the conditional to express a polite request:

Pourriez-vous m'aider ?	Could you help me?
Pourrais-je parler à M. Martin ?	May I speak to Mr. Martin?

Pouvoir can have different meanings in the past tenses. In the *passé composé*, it means "could" as in "was able to, managed to, succeeded in." In the imperfect, *pouvoir* also means "could" but does not indicate whether it actually happened.

Il a pu conduire.	He could (and did) drive.
Il pouvait conduire.	He could drive (he was capable).
Je n'ai pas pu décider.	I couldn't (and didn't) decide.
Je ne pouvais pas décider.	I couldn't decide (it was difficult).

In the past conditional, *pouvoir* means "could/might have done" (in terms of both ability and possibility):

Auriez-vous pu conduire ?	Could you have driven?
Il aurait pu tomber.	He might have fallen.

The impersonal construction *il se peut* means "it is possible" and is followed by the subjunctive:

Il se peut qu'il parte.	It is possible that he will leave./ He may leave.
Il se peut que je sois en retard.	It's possible that I'm late./ I might be late.

Peut-être means "perhaps" or "maybe":

Tu vas essayer ? Peut-être.	Are you going to try? Perhaps.
Nous allons peut-être dîner en ville.	We might have dinner in town.

Conjugations of *pouvoir*:

je	*peux*	*nous*	*pouvons*
tu	*peux*	*vous*	*pouvez*
il / elle	*peut*	*ils / elles*	*peuvent*

Essential

Savoir and Connaître—To Know

The verbs *savoir* and *connaître* are both translated by the English verb "to know." This might seem confusing to you at first, but once you learn the difference in meaning and usage for the two verbs you shouldn't have any trouble.

Savoir means to know:

- a fact
- how to do something

Savoir is often followed by an infinitive or a subordinate clause.

Je sais où il est.	I know where he is.
Sais-tu danser ?	Do you know how to dance?

Conjugations of *savoir:*

je	sais	nous	savons
tu	sais	vous	savez
il / elle	sait	ils / elles	savent

Connaître means:

- to know (someone)
- to be familiar with (someone or something)

Connaître always has a direct object.

Je connais tes frères.	I know your brothers.
Je connais cette histoire.	I am familiar with this story.
Nous connaissons la France.	We know/are familiar with France.

Conjugations for *connaître:*

je	connais	nous	connaissons
tu	connais	vous	connaissez
il / elle	connaît	ils / elles	connaissent

Venir—To Come

The irregular French verb *venir* means "to come" and is used just like its English equivalent.

Il vient demain.	He's coming tomorrow.
Je viens d'Espagne.	I'm from (I come from) Spain.

The verb *venir* is used to express *le passé récent*—the recent past. It is usually translated as "to have just (done something)." It is formed with *venir* conjugated into the present tense, followed by *de* and the infinitive of the action that has just occurred.

Je viens de manger.	I just ate.
Ils viennent de partir.	They just left.
Nous venons d'arriver.	We just arrived.

Venir conjugations:

je	viens	nous	venons
tu	viens	vous	venez
il / elle	vient	ils / elles	viennent

Vouloir—To Want

The French verb *vouloir* means "to want":

Je veux partir.	I want to leave.
Voulez-vous essayer?	Do you want to try?

 Fact

One of the most useful conjugations of *vouloir* is the first person singular (*je*) conditional, *voudrais*, which means "would like," as in: *Je voudrais un billet* (I'd like a ticket) and *Je voudrais partir demain* (I'd like to leave tomorrow).

Veuillez is the *vous* form of the imperative, used to express a very polite request:

Veuillez m'excuser.	Please (be so kind as to) excuse me.
Veuillez vous asseoir.	Please sit down.

Conjugations of *vouloir*:

je	veux	nous	voulons
tu	veux	vous	voulez
il / elle	veut	ils / elles	veulent

Exercices de contrôle

A. Translate the following verbs into English.

1. *venir* _____

2. *devoir* _____

3. *connaître* _____

4. *aller* _____

5. *être* _____

6. *faire* _____

7. *avoir* _____

8. *savoir* _____

9. *pouvoir* _____

10. *vouloir* _____

B. Translate each of these statements into French.

a. I have to know.

_____

b. He wants to come.

_____

c. We are going to eat.

_____

d. They know (are familiar with) Cannes.

_____

e. You (plural) can study.

_____

f. She has a brother.

_____

g. Are you (familiar) tired?

_____

h. He is right.

_____

i. How's the weather?

_____

j. You (plural) really have to come.

_____

Chapter 8

Simple Verb Tenses

A SIMPLE VERB TENSE is made up of a single conjugated verb, as opposed to a compound tense which has two verbs (an auxiliary and a participle). The present tense is the most common simple tense. Some other simple tenses are the imperfect, future, conditional, and simple past.

Imperfect—*l'imparfait*

The imperfect tense is used to talk about a past action or state of being without specifying when it began or ended. It is often equivalent to "was ___-ing" in English. The French imperfect is commonly used for descriptions, like *Il faisait chaud* (It was hot) and can also express repeated actions in the past, such as *Je lisais tous les jours* (I used to read every day).

The imperfect is relatively easy to conjugate, because all verbs—regular, stem-changing, and irregular—except *être* are conjugated the same way: by dropping the *-ons* from the present tense *nous* form and adding the appropriate ending.

je	-ais	nous	-ions
tu	-ais	vous	-iez
il / elle	-ait	ils / elles	-aient

Essential

Être is more regular in its imperfect form than in its present tense form. Use *ét-* as its stem and attach the regular imperfect endings to conjugate it in the imperfect tense, such as *"j'étais"* and *"vous étiez"*.

Here is an example of imperfect conjugations for *-er*, *-ir*, and *-re* verbs as well as *être*.

	PARLER	FINIR	RENDRE	ÊTRE
je (j')	parlais	finissais	rendais	étais
tu	parlais	finissais	rendais	étais
il / elle	parlait	finissait	rendait	était
nous	parlions	finissions	rendions	étions
vous	parliez	finissiez	rendiez	étiez
ils / elles	parlaient	finissaient	rendaient	étaient

Future and Conditional—*le futur et le conditionnel*

The French future and conditional are some of the easiest French conjugations. For most French verbs, including all regular *-er* and *-ir* verbs, the future and conditional are conjugated with the infinitive plus the appropriate endings. For regular *-re* verbs, the final *e* is dropped before the endings are added. The future/conditional stem, whether for a regular, stem-changing, or irregular verb, always ends in *r*.

Some stem-changing verbs have the same stem-change in the future and conditional as they do in the present tense. Below are rules for conjugating the imperfect for stem-changing verbs.

1. Verbs that end in *-yer* change the *y* to an *i* for the future and conditional stem (e.g., *paier-*, *nettoier-*)
2. Verbs that end in *-eler* double the *l* (*appeller-*, *renouveller-*) and verbs that end in *-eter* double the *t* (*jetter-*, *feuilletter-*).

3. Verbs that end in *-e_er* (where _ indicates any letter, with the exception of most *-eler* and *-eter* verbs) change the first *e* to *è* (*lève-*, *achète-*).

The following verbs have irregular future/conditional stems:

aller	ir-
avoir	aur-
devoir	devr-
envoyer	enverr-
être	ser-
faire	fer-
pleuvoir	pleuvr-
pouvoir	pourr-
savoir	saur-
venir	viendr-
voir	verr-
vouloir	voudr-

Future—*le futur*

The future tense indicates something that is going to happen in the future and is usually equivalent to "will" in English:

Ils étudieront plus tard.	They will study later.
J'irai à la banque demain.	I'll go to the bank tomorrow.

All verbs take the following endings for the future:

je	-ai	nous	-ons
tu	-as	vous	-ez
il / elle	-a	ils / elles	-ont

Examples of -*er*, -*ir*, -*re*, stem-changing, and irregular verbs in the future tense:

	PARLER	CHOISIR	RENDRE	LEVER	ALLER
je (j')	parlerai	choisirai	rendrai	lèverai	irai
tu	parleras	choisiras	rendras	lèveras	iras
il / elle	parlera	choisira	rendra	lèvera	ira
nous	parlerons	choisirons	rendrons	lèverons	irons
vous	parlerez	choisirez	rendrez	lèverez	irez
ils / elles	parleront	choisiront	rendront	lèveront	iront

Conditional—*le conditionnel*

The conditional is a verb mood used for actions that are not guaranteed to occur; often they are dependent on certain conditions. It is translated by "would" in English.

J'achèterais la chemise bleue.	I would buy the blue shirt.
Nous devrions partir à midi.	We would have to leave at noon.

The verb *vouloir* is used in the conditional to express a polite request:

Je voudrais un verre de vin.	I would like a glass of wine.
Je voudrais le faire moi-même.	I would like to do it myself.

The verb *aimer* is used in the conditional to express a polite desire, sometimes one that cannot be fulfilled:

J'aimerais bien le voir !	I would really like to see it/him!
Il aimerait jouer, mais il	He would like to play, but he
doit travailler.	has to work.

The conditional is conjugated with the infinitive or irregular conditional stem plus the conditional ending:

je	-ais	nous	-ions
tu	-ais	vous	-iez
il / elle	-ait	ils / elles	-aient

 **Alert!**

Remember that you can also express the future with the near future construction *aller* + infinitive, and that the conditional uses the exact same stems as the future; the only difference is in the ending.

Examples of *-er, -ir, -re*, stem-changing, and irregular verbs in the conditional:

	PARLER	CHOISIR	RENDRE	LEVER	ALLER
je (j')	parlerais	choisirais	rendrais	lèverais	irais
tu	parlerais	choisirais	rendrais	lèverais	irais
il / elle	parlerait	choisirait	rendrait	lèverait	irait
nous	parlerions	choisirions	rendrions	lèverions	irions
vous	parleriez	choisiriez	rendriez	lèveriez	iriez
ils / elles	parleraient	choisiraient	rendraient	lèveraient	iraient

Present Participle—*le participe présent*

The English present participle is the -ing form of a verb. The French present participle is formed by dropping *-ons* from the *nous* form of the present tense and adding *-ant*, for all but three verbs.

	PARLER	FINIR	VENDRE	DEVOIR
nous (présent)	parlons	finissons	vendons	devons
present participle	parlant	finissant	vendant	devant

The three exceptions are:

avoir	ayant
être	étant
savoir	sachant

For pronominal verbs, the present participle includes the reflexive pronoun.

se lever	s'habiller
se levant	s'habillant

Past Participle—le participe passé

The English past participle is the -ed or -en form of the verb. In French, the past participle of regular verbs is formed by dropping the infinitive ending of a verb and adding the past participle ending: *é* for-*er* verbs, *i* for -*ir* verbs, and *u* for -*re* verbs.

	PARLER	RÉUSSIR	VENDRE
remove	–er	–ir	–re
stem	parl–	réuss–	vend–
add	é	i	u
past participle	parlé	réussi	vendu

Most irregular verbs have irregular past participles:

apprendre	appris	avoir	eu
boire	bu	comprendre	compris
conduire	conduit	connaître	connu
construire	construit	courir	couru
craindre	craint	croire	cru

décevoir	déçu	devoir	dû
dire	dit	écrire	écrit
être	été	faire	fait
instruire	instruit	joindre	joint
lire	lu	mettre	mis
mourir	mort	offrir	offert
ouvrir	ouvert	naître	né
paraître	paru	peindre	peint
pouvoir	pu	prendre	pris
produire	produit	recevoir	reçu
savoir	su	souffrir	souffert
suivre	suivi	tenir	tenu
venir	venu	vivre	vécu
voir	vu	vouloir	voulu

The past participle has three main uses in French:

1. In conjunction with an auxiliary verb, the past participle forms compound tenses:

   J'ai étudié hier.   I studied yesterday.
   Il est arrivé à minuit.   He arrived at midnight.

2. With *être*, it forms the French passive voice.

   Le courrier est livré à deux heures.
   The mail is delivered at two o'clock.

   Cet enfant sera puni par ses parents.
   This child will be punished by his parents.

3. By itself or accompanied by *être*, the French past participle may serve as an adjective. Note that in some cases, the *participe passé* may be translated by the English present participle.

Déçu, j'ai pleuré pendant deux heures.
Disappointed, I cried for two hours.

La fille effrayée a crié.
The frightened girl screamed.

Le chien assis sur le canapé est à moi.
The dog sitting (seated) on the couch is mine.

Je ne vois pas l'enfant fatigué.
I don't see the tired child.

Ce livre est écrit en français.
This book is written in French.

Sais-tu si le film est terminé ?
Do you know if the movie is finished?

When the past participle is used in the passive voice or as an adjective, it needs to agree in gender and number with the word it modifies. In the compound tenses, it may or may not need to agree, depending on certain factors. You will learn agreement in Chapter 17.

Simple Past (Preterite)—*le passé simple*

The *passé simple* is a literary tense, meaning that it is used mainly in formal, written French (such as historical writing, literature, and journalism). In spoken French, the compound past (*le passé composé*), discussed in the next chapter of this book, is used instead. For this reason, you probably won't often need to conjugate the *passé simple*, but you should be able to recognize it.

The passé simple of *-er* verbs is formed by dropping *-er* and adding the *passé simple* endings:

je	-ai	nous	-âmes
tu	-as	vous	-âtes
il / elle	-a	ils / elles	-èrent

Thus to conjugate *parler*, you would remove *-er* to find the radical *parl-* and then add the appropriate endings:

je	parlai	nous	parlâmes
tu	parlas	vous	parlâtes
il / elle	parla	ils / elles	parlèrent

All *-er* verbs (including the irregular verb *aller*) are conjugated in this way, except for slight irregularities in verbs that end in *-ger* and *-cer*: for all grammatical persons except *ils / elles*, *e* is added after the stem of *-ger* verbs and *c* changes to *ç* in the stem of *-cer* verbs.

	MANGER	LANCER
je	mangeai	lançai
tu	mangeas	lanças
il / elle	mangea	lança
nous	mangeâmes	lançâmes
vous	mangeâtes	lançâtes
ils / elles	mangèrent	lancèrent

Regular *-ir* and *-re* verbs have the following simple past endings:

je	-is	nous	-îmes
tu	-is	vous	-îtes
il / elle	-it	ils / elles	-irent

Remove the *-ir* or *-re* and add the *passé simple* endings to get:

	FINIR	RENDRE
je	finis	rendis
tu	finis	rendis
il / elle	finit	rendit
nous	finîmes	rendîmes
vous	finîtes	rendîtes
ils / elles	finirent	rendirent

Exercices de contrôle

A. Conjugate the following verbs into the tense and grammatical person given in parentheses.

1. *hanter* (*tu*, imperfect) _____

2. *choisir* (*nous*, future) _____

3. *vendre* (*elle*, conditional) _____

4. *être* (*je*, imperfect) _____

5. *danser* (*vous*, future) _____

6. *finir* (*ils*, conditional) _____

7. *devoir* (*tu*, future) _____

8. *aller* (*il*, conditional) _____

9. *être* (*nous*, future) _____

10. *voir* (*elles*, conditional) _____

B. Provide the present and past participle for each of the following verbs.

a. *attendre*

_____

b. *étudier*

_____

c. *choisir*

_____

d. *aller*

_____

_____

e. *être*

_____

f. *avoir*

_____

g. *comprendre*

_____

h. *savoir*

_____

i. *pouvoir*

_____

j. *couper*

_____

Chapter 9

Compound Verb Tenses

COMPOUND VERB TENSES and moods are those made up of two parts: an auxiliary (helping) verb and a past participle. The auxiliary verb is what actually sets the tense and mood of the action—it must be conjugated according to the tense, mood, and voice of the action as well as to the subject.

Auxiliary Verbs—*les auxiliaires*

French has two auxiliary verbs used to conjugate the compound tenses, and all French verbs are classified by which auxiliary verb they take. Most French verbs use *avoir*, but the following verbs (and their derivatives) require *être*:

aller	to go
arriver	to arrive
descendre	to descend or to go down
entrer	to enter
monter	to climb or to go up
mourir	to die
naître	to be born
partir	to leave
passer	to spend (time)
rester	to stay
retourner	to return
sortir	to go out
tomber	to fall
venir	to come

These verbs, known as *être* verbs, are intransitive. However, when they are used transitively, the auxiliary verb changes to *avoir*.

Je suis monté hier.	I went up yesterday.
J'ai monté la valise.	I took the suitcase up.

In addition to the above verbs, all reflexive verbs take *être* in the compound tenses.

Compound Past Tense—*le passé composé*

The French *passé composé* is equivalent in English to the simple past (I ate) and the present perfect (I have eaten). In French, both of these sentences would be translated by *j'ai mangé*. The *passé composé* is the most common French past tense, often used in conjunction with the imperfect. It can express:

1. An action or state of being completed in the past:

As-tu nagé ce week-end ?	Did you swim this weekend?
Il est déjà parti.	He already left.

2. An action repeated a specific number of times in the past:

Hier, je suis tombé trois fois.	I fell three times yesterday.
Nous avons visité Paris plusieurs fois.	We've visited Paris several times.

3. A series of actions completed in the past:

    Il a vu sa mère, (a) parlé au médecin et (a) trouvé un chat.
    He saw his mother, talked to the doctor, and found a cat.

    Je suis allé à la banque et puis j'ai étudié.
    I went to the bank and then I studied.

The *passé composé* is often used in conjunction with the imperfect, as both express past actions and states of being but are used differently. While the imperfect is used to express ongoing actions with no specified completion, habitual or repeated actions, background information, and general descriptions, the *passé composé* denotes events with a definite beginning and end, single events, actions which interrupted something, and changes in physical or mental states. In general, the imperfect describes situations while the *passé composé* narrates events.

The *passé composé* is conjugated with the present tense of the appropriate auxiliary verb plus the past participle.

PARLER

j'	ai parlé	nous	avons parlé
tu	as parlé	vous	avez parlé
il / elle	a parlé	ils / elles	ont parlé

SORTIR

je	suis sorti(e)	nous	sommes sorti(e)s
tu	es sorti(e)	vous	êtes sorti(e)(s)
il / elle	est sorti(e)	ils / elles	sont sorti(e)s

LAVER

je	me suis lavé(e)	nous	nous sommes lavé(e)s
tu	t'es lavé(e)	vous	vous êtes lavé(e)(s)
il / elle	s'est lavé(e)	ils / elles	se sont lavé(e)s

The letters in parentheses indicate grammatical agreement—the conjugation depends on the word the verb is modifying.

Pluperfect (Past Perfect)— *le plus-que-parfait*

The French pluperfect is used to talk about an action in the past that occurred before another action in the past. The latter can be either mentioned in the same sentence or implied.

> *Il n'avait pas mangé (avant de sortir).*
> He hadn't eaten (before going out).

> *J'ai fait du shopping ce matin ; j'avais déjà fait la vaisselle.*
> I went shopping this morning; I had already done the dishes.

> *J'étais déjà sorti (quand tu as téléphoné).*
> I had already left (when you called).

> *Il voulait te parler parce qu'il ne t'avait pas vu hier.*
> He wanted to talk to you because he didn't see you yesterday.

 Essential

The pluperfect is also used in *si* clauses to express a hypothetical situation in the past that is contrary to what actually happened. An English example of this situation would be: "If she had asked the question, I would have agreed."

The pluperfect is conjugated with the imperfect of the appropriate auxiliary verb plus the past participle of the action verb.

j'	*avais parlé*	*nous*	*avions parlé*
tu	*avais parlé*	*vous*	*aviez parlé*
il / elle	*avait parlé*	*ils / elles*	*avaient parlé*

j'	*étais sorti(e)*	*nous*	*étions sorti(e)s*
tu	*étais sorti(e)*	*vous*	*étiez sorti(e)(s)*
il / elle	*était sorti(e)*	*ils / elles*	*étaient sorti(e)s*

je	*m'étais lavé(e)*	*nous*	*nous étions lavé(e)s*
tu	*t'étais lavé(e)*	*vous*	*vous étiez lavé(e)(s)*
il / elle	*s'était lavé(e)*	*ils / elles*	*s'étaient lavé(e)s*

Future perfect—*le futur antérieur*

The future perfect is mainly used to describe an action that will have happened by a specific point in the future.

J'aurai fini à trois heures.
I will have finished at three o'clock.

Quand tu rentreras, nous nous serons levés.
When you return home, we will have gotten up.

Je lui aurai dit demain.
I will have told him (by) tomorrow.

Dans une semaine, il sera né.
In a week, he will have been born.

The French future perfect can also be used to make simple assumptions about past events:

Elle n'est pas arrivée ; elle aura perdu le plan.
She hasn't arrived; she must have lost the map.

David s'est cassé la jambe ; il serait tombé.
David broke his leg; he must have fallen.

After the conjunctions *après que* (after), *aussitôt que* (as soon as), *dès que* (as soon as), *lorsque* (when), *quand* (when), and *une fois que* (once), the future perfect is used to express a future action which will be completed before another action, even though in English a present or past tense would follow:

Je le ferai une fois que j'aurai gagné de l'argent.
I will do it once I earn / have earned some money.

The French future perfect is conjugated with the auxiliary verb in the future plus the past participle.

j'	aurai aimé	nous	aurons aimé
tu	auras aimé	vous	aurez aimé
il / elle	aura aimé	ils / elles	auront aimé

je	serai venu(e)	nous	serons venu(e)s
tu	seras venu(e)	vous	serez venu(e)(s)
il / elle	sera venu(e)	ils / elles	seront venu(e)s

je	me serai lavé(e)	nous	nous serons lavé(e)s
tu	te seras lavé(e)	vous	vous serez lavé(e)(s)
il / elle	se sera lavé(e)	ils / elles	se seront lavé(e)s

Conditional Perfect (Past Conditional)— *le conditionnel parfait*

The French conditional perfect is used just like the English conditional perfect—to express actions that would have occurred in the past if circumstances had been different.

The conditional perfect is often used for the result clause in *si* clauses with the unmet condition in the pluperfect:

Si j'avais mangé, je ne me serais pas évanoui.
If I had eaten, I wouldn't have fainted.

Il serait tombé si tu l'avais poussé.
He would have fallen if you had pushed him.

(*Si* clauses are explained in detail in Chapter 15.)

The conditional perfect can be used to indicate a better alternative as to what actually happened in the past:

À votre place, je ne l'aurais pas fait.
In your place, I wouldn't have done it.

Tu aurais dû étudier.
You should have studied.

The conditional perfect can express an unrealized desire in the past:

J'aurais aimé y aller, mais ma mère a dit non.
I would have liked to go, but my mother said no.

Il aurait voulu voir le film, mais il n'avait pas d'argent.
He would have liked to see the movie, but he didn't have any money.

The conditional perfect can also report an uncertain or unverified statement, especially in the news:

Il y aurait eu des inondations à Calais.
Flooding in Calais has been reported.

Vingt maisons seraient détruites.
Apparently, twenty houses have been destroyed .

The conditional perfect is formed with the auxiliary verb conjugated into the conditional plus the past participle.

j'	*aurais aimé*	*nous*	*aurions aimé*
tu	*aurais aimé*	*vous*	*auriez aimé*
il / elle	*aurait aimé*	*ils / elles*	*auraient aimé*

je	*serais venu(e)*	*nous*	*serions venu(e)s*
tu	*serais venu(e)*	*vous*	*seriez venu(e)(s)*
il / elle	*serait venu(e)*	*ils / elles*	*seraient venu(e)s*

je	me serais lavé(e)	nous	nous serions lavé(e)s
tu	te serais lavé(e)	vous	vous seriez lavé(e)(s)
il / elle	se serait lavé(e)	ils / elles	se seraient lavé(e)s

Summary of Compound Tenses

Compound tenses are formed with the auxiliary verb conjugated into the tense/mood listed in the second column plus the past participle.

COMPOUND TENSE	AUXILIARY CONJUGATION	AVOIR VERB	ÊTRE VERB	REFLEXIVE VERB
Passé composé	Présent	j'ai mangé	je suis allé	je me suis habillé
Past perfect (pluperfect)	Imperfect	j'avais mangé	j'étais allé	je m'étais habillé
Future perfect	Future	j'aurai mangé	je serai allé	je me serai habillé
Past conditional	Conditional	j'aurais mangé	je serais allé	je me serais habillé

Exercices de contrôle

A. Conjugate the following verbs into all six masculine grammatical persons of the compound tense listed in parentheses.

1. *aimer (passé composé)*

   _____

2. *choisir (plus-que-parfait)*

   _____

3. *rendre (futur antérieur)*

   _____

4. *apprendre (plus-que-parfait)*

   _____

   _____

5. *pouvoir (futur antérieur)*

_____

6. *savoir (conditionnel parfait)*

_____

7. *sortir (plus-que-parfait)*

_____

8. *monter (passé composé)*

_____

9. *venir (conditionnel parfait)*

_____

10. *naître (passé composé)*

_____

11. *s'habiller (plus-que-parfait)*

_____

12. *se coucher (futur antérieur)*

_____

Chapter 10

Mood and Voice

MOOD AND VOICE are two more things you need to consider when conjugating verbs. Along with tense and grammatical person, mood and voice provide information about the verb and the subject performing it. Mood provides the feeling of a verb; that is, the speaker's attitude or feeling toward the action being expressed. Is the action factual or doubtful, a possibility or a command? Voice, on the other hand, indicates the relationship between the subject and the verb: who is performing the action on whom.

Introduction to Mood

Mood is the grammatical term for verb inflections (conjugations) that indicate how the speaker feels about the action/state of the verb; that is, how likely or factual the statement is. The French language has six moods that can be grouped into two categories: personal moods and impersonal moods.

Personal moods:
1. *Indicatif*   Indicative
2. *Subjonctif*   Subjunctive
3. *Conditionnel*   Conditional
4. *Impératif*   Imperative

Impersonal moods:
5. *Participe*   Participle
6. *Infinitif*   Infinitive

Fact

Personal moods make a distinction between grammatical persons—
they are conjugated. Impersonal moods do not distinguish between
grammatical persons and thus are not conjugated—they have a single form for all persons.

The indicative is what you might call the "normal" mood, as it is
by far the most common. It is used when the speaker wants to indicate a fact or ask a question. All of the conjugations you have learned
so far in this book are in the indicative with the exception of the conditional, conditional perfect, and present and past participles.

Imperative—l'impératif

The imperative is the verb mood used to give a command, either
affirmative (Go!) or negative (Don't go!). There are only three forms
of the imperative (*tu*, *nous*, and *vous*) and their conjugations are
among the easiest in French.

The imperative for all three forms of nearly all *-ir* and *-re* verbs
(regular and irregular) is the same as the present tense of the indicative. In addition, the *nous* and *vous* forms of -er verbs is the same
in the indicative and imperative. However, the imperative for the *tu*
form of *-er* verbs as well as verbs like *ouvrir* which are conjugated
like *-er* verbs (meaning that in the indicative the *tu* form ends in -
es), is a little different: the final *s* is dropped to make the imperative:
tu manges (you eat) becomes *mange* (eat).

Examples of the French imperative:

	PARLER	*FINIR*	*ATTENDRE*
(tu)	*parle*	*finis*	*attends*
(nous)	*parlons*	*finissons*	*attendons*
(vous)	*parlez*	*finissez*	*attendez*

Essential

In the French imperative, the subject pronoun is dropped, just as it is in English. You can just as clearly communicate "You go!" by simply saying, "Go!".

There are only four verbs with irregular forms in the imperative:

	AVOIR	*ÊTRE*	*SAVOIR*	*VOULOIR*
(tu)	*aie*	*sois*	*sache*	*veuille*
(nous)	*ayons*	*soyons*	*sachons*	*n/a*
(vous)	*ayez*	*soyez*	*sachez*	*veuillez*

Reflexive verbs in the imperative are followed by their reflexive pronoun and joined by a hyphen.

se lever	*s'habiller*
lève-toi	*habille-toi*
levons-nous	*habillons-nous*
levez-vous	*habillez-vous*

Subjunctive—*le subjonctif*

The subjunctive mood is subjective: it expresses emotional, potential, and hypothetical attitudes about what is being expressed—things like will/wanting, emotion, doubt, possibility, necessity, and judgment. The subjunctive is required after many verbs, conjunctions, and impersonal expressions.

Je veux que tu viennes.	I want you to come.
J'ai peur qu'il soit malade.	I'm afraid he is sick.
Il travaille pour que je puisse étudier.	He works so that I can study.

Elle pleure bien qu'elle *ne soit pas triste.*	She is crying even though she's not sad.
Il est possible que nous venions.	It's possible that we will come.
Il est bon que tu saches la vérité.	It's good that you know the truth.

The subjunctive endings are the same for regular, stem-changing, and irregular verbs, but the stem varies. For regular *-er*, *-ir*, and *-re* verbs, start with the present tense, third person plural form (*ils / elles*), drop the *-ent* ending to find the subjunctive stem, and add the following subjunctive endings:

	ENDING	*PARLER*	*CHOISIR*	*RENDRE*
... que je	-e	*parle*	*choisisse*	*rende*
... que tu	-es	*parles*	*choisisses*	*rendes*
... qu'il / elle	-e	*parle*	*choisisse*	*rende*
... que nous	-ions	*parlions*	*choisissions*	*rendions*
... que vous	-iez	*parliez*	*choisissiez*	*rendiez*
... qu'ils / elles	-ent	*parlent*	*choisissent*	*rendent*

Subjunctive conjugations of verbs are used for both the present and future—there is no future subjunctive. Stem-changing verbs and many irregular verbs follow the same pattern as regular verbs for the singular conjugations (*je*, *tu*, *il / elle*) as well as the third person plural (*ils / elles*). But for the *nous* and *vous* forms of the subjunctive, they use the first person plural (*nous*) as the stem:

	ENVOYER	*JETER*	*PRENDRE*	*VENIR*
... que je (j')	*envoie*	*jette*	*prenne*	*vienne*
... que tu	*envoies*	*jettes*	*prennes*	*viennes*
... qu'il / elle	*envoie*	*jette*	*prenne*	*vienne*
... que nous	*envoyions*	*jetions*	*prenions*	*venions*
... que vous	*envoyiez*	*jetiez*	*preniez*	*veniez*
... qu'ils / elles	*envoient*	*jettent*	*prennent*	*viennent*

Other irregular verbs which follow this pattern are *boire, croire, devoir, mourir, recevoir,* and *voir.*

Aller and *vouloir* each have two irregular stems but follow the above pattern and take the same endings.

	ALLER	VOULOIR
. . . que je (j')	*aille*	*veuille*
. . . que tu	*ailles*	*veuilles*
. . . qu'il / elle	*aille*	*veuille*
. . . que nous	*allions*	*voulions*
. . . que vous	*alliez*	*vouliez*
. . . qu'ils / elles	*aillent*	*veuillent*

Three verbs have a single irregular stem but use the same endings:

	FAIRE	POUVOIR	SAVOIR
. . . que je (j')	*fasse*	*puisse*	*sache*
. . . que tu	*fasses*	*puisses*	*saches*
. . . qu'il / elle	*fasse*	*puisse*	*sache*
. . . que nous	*fassions*	*puissions*	*sachions*
. . . que vous	*fassiez*	*puissiez*	*sachiez*
. . . qu'ils / elles	*fassent*	*puissent*	*sachent*

Avoir and *être* are completely irregular in the subjunctive.

. . . que je (j')	*aie*	*sois*
. . . que tu	*aies*	*sois*
. . . qu'il / elle	*ait*	*soit*
. . . que nous	*ayons*	*soyons*
. . . que vous	*ayez*	*soyez*
. . . qu'ils / elles	*aient*	*soient*

Past Subjunctive

There are two different past subjunctives. They are used for the same reasons as the present subjunctive—to express emotion, doubt, etc., but in the past. Once you understand how to use the present subjunctive, you should have no trouble with the past subjunctives.

Past Subjunctive—*le subjonctif passé*

The past subjunctive is used when a verb requiring the subjunctive in the subordinate clause (the verb that follows *que*) happened before the verb in the main clause.

The main clause may be in the present tense with the subordinate clause in the past.

Je suis heureuse que tu aies réussi.	I'm happy that you succeeded.
Nous avons peur qu'il soit mort.	We're afraid that he died.

Or both the main clause and the subordinate clause may be in the past tense.

Je doutas que vous l'ayez fait.	I doubted that you had done it.
J'avais peur que tu aies oublié.	I was afraid that you had forgotten.

 Essential

In the sentence *Je doutas que vous l'ayez fait* (I doubted that you had done it), if the main clause did not call for the subjunctive, the subordinate clause would have been in the pluperfect, because the subordinate clause happened before the verb in the main clause: *Je savais que vous l'aviez fait* (I knew you had done it).

The past subjunctive is formed with the present subjunctive of the auxiliary verb plus the past participle of the main verb.

j'	*aie parlé*	*nous*	*ayons parlé*
tu	*aies parlé*	*vous*	*ayez parlé*
il / elle	*ait parlé*	*ils / elles*	*aient parlé*

je	*sois allé(e)*	*nous*	*soyons allé(e)s*
tu	*sois allé(e)*	*vous*	*soyez allé(e)(s)*
il / elle	*soit allé(e)*	*ils / elles*	*soient allé(e)s*

je	*me sois levé(e)*	*nous*	*nous soyons levé(e)s*
tu	*te sois levé(e)*	*vous*	*vous soyez levé(e)(s)*
il / elle	*se soit levé(e)*	*ils / elles*	*se soient levé(e)s*

Imperfect Subjunctive— *l'imparfait du subjonctif*

The imperfect subjunctive is a literary tense like the *passé simple* but is even rarer. The imperfect subjunctive of *-er* verbs is formed with the third person singular form of the *passé simple* as the stem plus the imperfect subjunctive endings.

	ENDINGS	IMPERFECT SUBJUNCTIVE OF *PARLER*
... que je	*-sse*	*parlasse*
... que tu	*-sses*	*parlasses*
... qu'il / elle	*-^t*	*parlât*
... que nous	*-ssions*	*parlassions*
... que vous	*-ssiez*	*parlassiez*
... qu'ils / elles	*-ssent*	*parlassent*

All *-er* verbs (including the normally irregular verb *aller*) are conjugated according to this pattern.

For *-ir* verbs, *-re* verbs, and irregular verbs, the stem of the imperfect subjunctive is formed with the third person singular form of the *passé simple* minus the final *t*, plus the imperfect subjunctive endings.

	ENDINGS	FINIR	RENDRE	AVOIR	VENIR
...que je (j')	-sse	finisse	rendisse	eusse	vinsse
...que tu	-sses	finisses	rendisses	eusses	vinsses
...qu'il / elle	-^t	finît	rendît	eût	vînt
...que nous	-ssions	finissions	rendissions	eussions	vinssions
...que vous	-ssiez	finissiez	rendissiez	eussiez	vinssiez
...qu'ils / elles	-ssent	finissent	rendissent	eussent	vinssent

 Question?

Since the imperfect subjunctive is a literary tense, do you need to know how to conjugate it?
You will probably never need to conjugate it yourself, but in order to recognize it, you need to learn how it is conjugated.

Voice—*la voix*

Voice indicates the relationship between the subject and verb—who is performing the action on whom. There are three French voices:

1. **Active**—The subject performs the action of the verb. Active is the most typical, "normal" voice.

Je répare la voiture.	I'm repairing the car.
Il habille le bébé.	He's dressing the baby.

2. **Passive**—The action of the verb is performed on the subject by an agent.

La voiture est réparée.	The car is (being) repaired.
La souris est mangée par le chat.	The mouse is eaten by the cat.

3. Reflexive—The subject performs the action on itself.

Je me lave.	I'm washing up.
Il s'habille.	He's getting dressed.

Everything you've seen so far in this book has been in the active voice, with the exception of pronominal verbs (reflexive voice) in Chapter 5. Now you need to understand passive voice.

The passive voice is formed with *être* conjugated into the appropriate tense, followed by the past participle. It exists in all tenses and moods as you can see here with *faire le lit* (to make the bed). However, it is not very commonly used.

	ACTIVE	PASSIVE
present	*je fais le lit*	*le lit est fait par moi*
passé composé	*j'ai fait le lit*	*le lit a été fait par moi*
imperfect	*je faisais le lit*	*le lit était fait par moi*
future	*je ferai le lit*	*le lit sera fait par moi*
subjunctive	*… que je fasse le lit*	*… que le lit soit fait par moi*

The passive voice always has one more verb (the auxiliary verb *être*) than the active voice. In the passive voice, the action described by the verb is being done to the subject by an agent, which may or may not be stated.

ACTIVE VOICE	PASSIVE VOICE
Quelqu'un fait le ménage.	*Le ménage est fait.*
On le respecte.	*Il est respecté.*
Jacques fait le ménage.	*Le ménage est fait par Jacques.*
Un enfant lit le livre.	*Le livre est lu par un enfant.*
Mes amis aiment mon père.	*Mon père est aimé de mes amis.*
Tout le monde le respecte.	*Il est respecté de tout le monde.*

In the first two examples, the agent is impersonal. In the third and fourth examples, the verb is expressing an action, and the agent is introduced by the preposition *par*. In the last two examples, the verb expresses a state of being and the agent is introduced by *de*.

Even more so than in English, it is preferable to avoid the passive voice in French, which has a slightly formal or literary tone. There are several ways to avoid it.

1. Turn the agent into a subject and use the active voice:

    Ce livre a été écrit par une femme.   Une femme a écrit ce livre.
    This book was written by a woman. A woman wrote this book.

2. Put the agent at the beginning of the sentence, preceded by *c'est*:

    Ce livre a été écrit par une femme.   C'est une femme qui a écrit ce livre.
    This book was written by a woman. It was a woman who wrote this book.

3. Use *on* as the subject:

    Ce livre a été écrit en 2005.   On a écrit ce livre en 2005.
    This book was written in 2005. Someone wrote this book in 2005.

Exercices de contrôle

A. Provide the conjugations of all grammatical persons for the following verbs in the mood in parentheses.

1. *danser* (imperative)

    _____

2. *finir* (present subjunctive)

    _____

3. *vendre* (past subjunctive)

_____

4. *réussir* (imperative)

_____

5. *chanter* (present subjunctive)

_____

6. *étudier* (past subjunctive)

_____

7. *être* (imperative)

_____

8. *savoir* (present subjunctive)

_____

9. *descendre* (past subjunctive)

_____

10. *faire* (present subjunctive)

_____

B. Rewrite the following passive voice statements using the active voice. If there is no agent, use the word in parentheses as the subject.

a. *Le jus a été bu par David.*

_____

b. *Mon chat est lavé. (je)*

_____

c. *Le balcon a été construit par deux hommes.*

_____

d. *Le jardin est recouvert de neige.*

_____

e. *Votre frère a été retrouvé. (on)*

_____

f. *Son père est admiré de tout le monde.*

_____

g. *Le document a été écrit hier. (ils)*

_____

h. *Ton livre a été acheté par des enfants.*

_____

i. *Le salon est rempli de meubles.*

_____

j. *J'ai été appelé hier. (on)*

_____

Chapter 11

Questions

ASKING QUESTIONS can be difficult in any language, because there are usually several different types of interrogative constructions, special interrogatory words may be required, and the word order is usually different for questions and statements. All of these difficulties are present in French. This chapter will teach you how to use the different ways to ask questions in French, including both the grammatically proper form of questioning and the more common ways to ask questions.

Introduction to Questions

There are four ways to ask questions in French. Below are the four different constructions, listed in order, from formal to informal.

1. Invert the subject and verb and join them with a hyphen.

Comprends-tu ?	Do you understand?
As-tu compris ?	Did you understand?

2. Put *est-ce que* at the beginning of any sentence:

Est-ce que tu comprends ?	Do you understand?
Est-ce que tu as compris ?	Did you understand?

3. Add the tag *n'est-ce pas* to the end of the sentence (when you expect the answer to be yes):

Tu comprends, n'est-ce pas ?   You understand, right?
Tu as compris, n'est-ce pas ?   You understood, right?

4. Raise the pitch of your voice at the end of any sentence:

Tu comprends ?   You understand?
Tu as compris ?   You understood?

The first two constructions are the "correct" ways to ask questions. In French, as in any other language, there is a difference between the grammatically correct way to say things, and the way that things are actually said. Inversion and *est-ce que* are the proper ways to ask, while the *n'est-ce pas* tag and the raised pitch are both typical of informal speech.

 Essential

A dual-verb construction occurs whenever you have a conjugated verb followed by an infinitive. Verbs commonly used in this construction are *aller, devoir, pouvoir,* and *vouloir.*

Inversion can only be done when the subject is a pronoun: *doit-il ? veux-tu ? aimez-vous ?* When inversion is used with a verb that ends in *e* followed by the pronouns *il* or *elle, t-* must be added.

Aime-t-il le fromage ?   Does he like cheese?
Étudie-t-elle tous les jours ?   Does she study every day?
Chante-t-il ?   Does he sing?

With compound conjugations and dual-verb constructions, inversion takes place between the pronoun and the first verb, followed by the past participle or second verb.

As-tu mangé ?	Have you eaten?
Est-il monté ?	Did he go up?
Veux-tu danser ?	Do you want to dance?
Vont-ils étudier ?	Are they going to study?

Yes—No Questions

Questions to which the answer is yes or no are the simplest. You can use any of the above constructions and you can answer with a simple *oui* or *non*, or by restating the question as a statement.

Question:

Aimes-tu danser ? Est-ce que tu aimes danser ?	Do you like to dance?

Possible answers:

Oui.	Yes.
Oui, j'aime danser.	Yes, I like to dance.
Non.	No.
Non, je n'aime pas danser.	No, I don't like to dance.

 Fact

Comment ? in this context means "What?" or "I beg your pardon." Use this word when you did not hear or understand what another person said. It can be especially useful when traveling in France!

In French, there is a special word used to respond to negative questions and statements. Whereas in English, if someone says to you "Aren't you coming?" and you respond "Yes," there is some ambiguity. Are you saying "Yes, that's right, I'm not coming," or are you saying "Yes, I am coming"? In French, this ambiguity does not exist, thanks to the word *si*, which is used when you want to contradict a negation.

Tu ne viens pas ?	Aren't you coming?
Si.	Yes (I am coming).
N'as-tu pas mangé ?	Haven't you eaten?
Si.	Yes (I have eaten).
Tu ne dois pas travailler demain.	You don't have to work tomorrow.
Si.	Yes (I do).
Marc, veux-tu jouer ?	Marc, do you want to play?
Oui !	Yes!
Dommage, tu ne peux pas.	Too bad, you can't.
Si !	Yes (I can)!

Interrogative Adverbs

Interrogative adverbs are used to ask for new information or facts, whereas regular interrogative questions lead to a "yes" or "no" answer. These useful words will help you elicit more detailed information about a subject.

Common French interrogative adverbs

combien de	how many/much
comment	how
où	where
pourquoi	why
quand	when

All of these can be used with either *est-ce que* or inversion. Examples of asking the same question using both *est-ce que* and inversion:

Combien de livres veut-il ?/Combien de livres est-ce qu'il veut ?
How many books does he want?

Comment as-tu fait cela ?/Comment est-ce que tu as fait cela ?
How did you do that?

Où habites-tu ?/Où est-ce que tu habites ?
Where do you live?

Pourquoi chantez-vous ?/Pourquoi est-ce que vous chantez ?
Why are you singing?

Quand manges-tu ?/Quand est-ce que tu manges ?
When do you eat?

Interrogative Adjectives

When it comes to interrogative adjectives, French grammar is much more strict than English grammar. In English, you can say "What book do you want?" and no one will raise an eyebrow, though technically it is grammatically incorrect. In proper English, the question should be "Which book do you want?" but in reality, "what book" is much more common. In French, however, you do not have this option: the French equivalent of which, *quel*, must be used whenever there is more than one noun that you are choosing between—thus, "*Quel livre?*" *Quel* + noun is replaced by the interrogative pronoun *lequel*. *Quel livre veux-tu ? Lequel veux-tu ?*

Basically, *quel* is used whenever you want specific information about a noun.

Quel document as-tu lu ?	What (which) document did you read?
Quelle heure est-il ?	What time is it?
Dans quel magasin travaille-t-il ?	What store does he work at or for?

- Ana m'a prêté une voiture.   Ana loaned me a car.
- Quelle voiture ?   What (which) car?

 Alert!

Remember that *quel* has to agree in gender and number with the noun it modifies, and that it is also an exclamative adjective: *Quel bateau !* (What a boat!)

Quel can be used with inversion or *est-ce que*:

Quel verre veux-tu ?   What glass do you want?
Quel verre est-ce que tu veux ?   What glass do you want?
Quelle heure est-il ?   What time is it?

Quel can be used after a preposition:

À quelle heure va-t-il arriver ?   What time is he going to arrive?
De quels étudiants est-ce qu'il parle ?   What students is he talking about?

Quel followed by *être*:

Quel est le problème ?   What's the problem?
Quelle est votre question ?   What's your question?

Interrogative Pronouns

Interrogative pronouns ask "who," "what," or "which one." The three French interrogative pronouns are *qui*, *que*, and *lequel* and all three of these can also be relative pronouns. (See Chapter 15 for more information on relative pronouns.)

Qui means "who" or "whom" and is used to ask about people.

Qui êtes-vous ?	Who are you?
Qui est là ?	Who's there?

When "whom" is the object of the question, *qui* can be followed by either *est-ce que* or inversion.

Qui est-ce que vous aimez ? Qui aimez-vous ?	Whom do you love?
Qui est-ce qu'il a vu ? Qui a-t-il vu ?	Whom did he see?

 Fact

Although "whom" is the grammatically correct term in English, it is not uncommon to hear "who" in this type of construction—who do you love? who did he see?

When "who" is the subject of the question, you can use either *qui* or *qui est-ce qui*. The word order cannot be inverted and the verb is always in the third person singular.

Qui (est-ce qui) veut étudier le français ?	Who wants to study French?
Qui (est-ce qui) vient avec nous ?	Who is coming with us?

When *qui* follows a preposition, you can use inversion or *est-ce que*.

À qui est-ce que tu parles ? À qui parles-tu ?
To whom are you speaking?

Pour qui est-ce qu'il a travaillé ? Pour qui a-t-il travaillé ?
Whom did he work for?

Que means "what" and is used to refer to ideas or objects. When "what" is the object of the question, it can be followed by inversion or *est-ce que*.

Qu'est-ce qu'elle cherche ? Que cherche-t-elle ?
What is she looking for?

Qu'est-ce que tu penses de cette idée ? Que penses-tu de cette idée ?
What do you think of this idea?

Qu'est-ce que c'est (que cela) ?
What is that?

When "what" is the subject of the question, *qu'est-ce qui* must be used, followed by a third person singular verb, with no inversion.

Qu'est-ce qui se passe ?   What's happening?
Qu'est-ce qui a pu faire cela ?   What could have done this?

After a preposition, *que* changes to *quoi*.

Avec quoi est-ce que vous écrivez ? Avec quoi écrivez-vous ?
What are you writing with?

À quoi est-ce que tu penses ? À quoi penses-tu ?
What are you thinking about?

Lequel usually means *which one* and is a bit more complicated, for two reasons.

1. It has to agree in gender and number with the noun it replaces:

	SINGULAR	PLURAL
masculine	*lequel*	*lesquels*
feminine	*laquelle*	*lesquelles*

2. Like the definite articles *le* and *les*, *lequel* and its plural forms must form a contraction when preceded by the prepositions *à* and *de*:

À + LEQUEL		DE + LEQUEL	
auquel	*auxquels*	*duquel*	*desquels*
à laquelle	*auxquelles*	*de laquelle*	*desquelles*

As an interrogative pronoun, *lequel* replaces *quel* + noun.

Quel sandwich veux-tu ?	Which sandwich do you want?
Lequel veux-tu ? (Quel sandwich ?)	Which one do you want?
Je veux la jupe là-bas.	I want the skirt over there.
Laquelle ? (Quelle jupe ?)	Which one?
Je pense à mon ami.	I'm thinking about my friend.
Auquel penses-tu ? (À quel ami ?)	Which one are you thinking about?

Summary of interrogative pronouns:

	SUBJECT OF QUESTION	OBJECT OF QUESTION	AFTER PREPOSITION
	qui	*qui*	*qui*
Who	*qui est-ce qui*	*qui est-ce que*	
What	*qu'est-ce qui*	*que*	*quoi*
		qu'est-ce que	
Which	*lequel*	*lequel*	*lequel, laquelle,* etc.
			auquel, à laquelle
			duquel, de laquelle

Exercices de contrôle

A. Turn each of the following statements into two questions—one with *est-ce que* and the other with inversion.

   1. *Tu aimes les livres.*

   _____

   2. *Il croit tout.*

   _____

   3. *Vous partirez à midi.*

   _____

   4. *Elles savent la vérité.*

   _____

   5. *Elle aime lire.*

   _____

   6. *Ils parlent français.*

   _____

   7. *Nous aimons voyager.*

   _____

   8. *Vous êtes allés en France.*

   _____

   9. *Il a mangé avec nous.*

   _____

   10. *Elle adore regarder les films.*

   _____

B. Translate the following into French.

a. Hasn't he arrived yet? Yes (he has).

_____

b. Don't you want to eat? Yes (I do).

_____

c. Where does she work?

_____

d. Why do you hate apples?

_____

e. How many cousins do they have?

_____

f. Which man said hello?

_____

g. Who speaks French?

_____

h. Whom did you see?

_____

i. What do they want?

_____

j. I want a cat (*un chat*). Which one?

_____

Chapter 12

Negation

NO MATTER HOW positive and optimistic you are, sometimes you just have to say no. In this chapter, you'll learn all about how to be grammatically negative in French. There are a variety of ways to make a statement negative in French, and each construction is used for specific situations. With a little practice, you will be able to respond easily with the proper form of negation.

Ne . . . pas and Other Negative Adverbs

Negative adverbs are the constructions used to negate the action or state of a verb. The English negative adverb is "not," as in "I'm not going, I don't (do not) have time." In French, it's a little bit more complicated.

The French equivalent of "not" is the two-part construction *ne . . . pas*, which surrounds the verb being negated. To make a sentence or question negative, place *ne* in front of the conjugated verb and *pas* after it.

Je suis grand—Je ne suis pas grand.
I'm tall—I'm not tall.

Vous êtes fatigué ?—Vous n'êtes pas fatigué ?
Are you tired?—Aren't you tired?

In dual-verb and compound tense constructions, *ne . . . pas* surrounds the conjugated verb.

Il veut jouer—Il ne veut pas jouer.
He wants to play—He doesn't want to play.

J'ai mangé—Je n'ai pas mangé.
I ate—I didn't eat.

When negating an infinitive, *ne pas* stays together in front of the verb: *J'ai décidé de ne pas accepter.* (I decided not to accept.) *Ne . . . pas* is the most common negative adverb, but there are a number of others, all of which follow the above placement rules.

ne . . . pas encore	not yet
Il n'a pas encore mangé.	He hasn't eaten yet.
ne . . . pas toujours	not always
Je ne mange pas toujours ici.	I don't always eat here.
ne . . . pas du tout	not at all
Je n'aime pas du tout cette idée.	I don't like this idea at all.
ne . . . plus	no more, not anymore
Vous n'écrivez plus ?	You don't write anymore?
ne . . . jamais	never
Il ne voyage jamais.	He never travels.
ne . . . que	only
Il n'y a qu'un chat.	There is only one cat.

Essential

Remember that when there is an indefinite or partitive article in a negative construction, it changes to *de*, meaning "any." *J'ai une pomme—Je n'ai pas de pomme*. (I have an apple—I don't have any apples).

Ne Without Pas

Though *ne . . . pas* is used most commonly as a pair, there are two types of constructions in which *ne* is used without *pas*. Both of them are formal and are more common in written than spoken French, so you should be able to recognize them though you may or may not need to use them yourself.

Ne explétif

The *ne explétif* is a "non-negative" *ne* that is used after certain verbs, conjunctions, and comparatives. It doesn't make the verb negative, but rather is used in situations where the main clause has a negative (either bad or negated) meaning, such as expressions of fear, warning, doubt, and negation. The important thing is to recognize the *ne explétif* so that when you do see or hear it, you understand that it does not negate the subordinate clause.

Here are some common French words that expect the *ne explétif*.

Verbs: *avoir peur* (to be afraid), *craindre* (to fear), *douter* (to doubt), *empêcher* (to prevent), *éviter* (to avoid), *nier* (to deny)

Conjunctions: *à moins que* (unless), *avant que* (before), *de crainte que* (for fear that), *de peur que* (for fear that), *plutôt que* (rather than)

Comparatives: *autre* (other), *meilleur* (better), *mieux* (best), *moins* (less), *pire* (worse), *plus* (more).

If the subordinate clause is supposed to have a negative (negated) meaning, just use *ne . . . pas* as usual (examples in parentheses).

Elle craint qu'il ne revienne.
She's afraid that he will come back.

*(Elle craint qu'il ne revienne **pas**.)*
(She's afraid that he *won't* come back.)

Je n'y vais pas de peur qu'il ne soit là.
I'm not going for fear that he will be there.

*(je n'y vais pas de peur qu'il ne soit **pas** là.)*
(I'm not going for fear that he *won't* be there.)

C'est facile à moins que tu ne sois faible.
It's easy unless you're weak.

*(C'est facile à moins que tu ne sois **pas** fort.)*
(It's easy unless you're *not* strong.)

Literary *Ne*

The literary *ne* occurs in literary writing (and, to a much lesser extent, spoken French) with certain verbs and constructions that need *ne* but not *pas* in order to be negative.

The three verbs that don't need *pas* are:

cesser	*Il ne cesse de parler.*	He never stops talking.
oser	*Je n'ose le dire.*	I don't dare say it.
pouvoir	*Elle ne peut partir.*	She can't leave.

Note that the use of *pas* in these constructions is not prohibited, simply optional. *Savoir* is a special case, as it can be used without *pas* only in certain constructions. It doesn't need *pas* when it means "to be uncertain":

Je ne sais si je dois le faire.   I don't know if I should do it.

Savoir also doesn't need *pas* when it is in the conditional:

Je ne saurais t'aider. I wouldn't know how to help you.

However, *savoir* does need *pas* when it means to know a fact or how to do something:

Je ne sais pas la réponse. I don't know the answer.
Il ne sait pas nager. He doesn't know how to swim.

Pas Without *Ne*

There are also two types of situations in which *pas* is used without *ne*, including informal negation and non-verbal negation.

Informal Negation

On the opposite end of the spectrum from the formal negative structures in the previous section, you have informal French, in which *ne* is often dropped, leaving only *pas* to make the statement negative. Although *ne* is nearly always written, it is often dropped in spoken French.

Je ne suis pas prêt—Je suis pas prêt. I'm not ready.
Tu ne peux pas y aller ? Tu peux pas y aller ? You can't go?
Ne mange pas ça !—Mange pas ça ! Don't eat that!
Je n'ai jamais fait ça.—J'ai jamais fait ça. I've never done that.

Non-verbal Negation

When negating an adjective, adverb, noun, or some other non-verbal construction, *pas* is used on its own, paired with an adjective, adverb, noun or pronoun.

Pas + adjective
Pas parfait, mais ça marche. Not perfect, but it works.
Pas bon, ça. That's not good.
C'est un garçon pas gentil. He is an unkind boy.

Pas + adverb

Pas trop.	Not too much.
Pas mal.	Not bad.
Pourquoi pas ?	Why not?

Pas + noun

Tu viens demain ?	Are you coming tomorrow?
Non, pas demain. lundi.	No, not tomorrow. Monday.
Pas de problème !	No problem!

Pas + pronoun

J'ai faim, pas toi ?	I'm hungry, aren't you?
Pas moi !	Not me!
Pas ceci ; je veux cela.	Not this; I want that.

Pas can also be used to confirm a statement.

Tu comprends, ou pas ?	Do you understand, or not?
Je veux le faire, pas toi ?	I want to do it, don't you?
Pas juste ?	Right? Isn't that correct?

Fact

Using *pas* to confirm a statement can be somewhat informal. If you are speaking in a formal situation, you should try to reword the sentence to negate a verb with *ne . . . pas*, rather than using one of these informal constructions.

Saying Yes and No

Like English, French has words for yes and no: *oui* and *non*. Unlike English, French has a special word, *si*, that is used only when responding yes to a negative question.

Veux-tu jouer?	Do you want to play?
Oui!	Yes!
Veux-tu jouer?	Do you want to play?
Non!	No!
Ne veux-tu pas jouer?	Don't you want to play?
Si!	Yes (I do)!
Ne veux-tu pas jouer?	Don't you want to play?
Non!	No (that's correct, I don't)!

Negative Adjectives

Like negative adverbs, French negative adjectives are composed of two words which surround the verb. Negative adjectives negate, refuse, or cast doubt on a quality of the noun they modify.

Vous n'avez aucune preuve.	You don't have any proof.
Je ne connais pas un seul avocat.	I don't know a single lawyer.
Pas un problème n'a été résolu.	No problem has been resolved.

There are four French negative adjectives:

ne . . . aucun(e)	no, not any
ne . . . nul(le)	no, not any
ne . . . pas un(e)	no, not one
ne . . . pas un(e) seul(e)	not a single

All of these mean more or less the same thing, with *ne . . . pas un seul* being just a bit stronger. However, *pas un* and *pas un seul* are used only for countable nouns (people, cars), *nul* is only for collective nouns (money, time), and *aucun* can be used for both countable and collective nouns.

The parentheses indicate the letters that need to be added when negating a feminine noun because, like all adjectives, negative adjectives must agree in gender and number with the nouns that they modify. When a negative adjective modifies the subject of the sentence, the verb must be conjugated in the third person singular.

Pas une seule femme ne le sait.	Not a single woman knows it.
Aucune femme ne le veut.	No woman wants it.
Aucun argent n'a été retrouvé.	No money was found.

 Essential

Remember that an indefinite article in a negative construction normally changes to *de*. However, you can also use *pas un(e)*, with a slight difference in nuance:

Je n'ai pas de pomme (I don't have any apples) is a general statement.
Je n'ai pas une pomme (I don't have a single apple) stresses the negative.

Negative Pronouns

Like adjectives and adverbs, French negative pronouns consist of two parts which surround the verb. Negative pronouns are used to negate, refuse, or cast doubt on the existence of the noun that they replace.

Elles n'ont vu aucun des films.	They haven't seen any of the movies.
Je n'ai rien fait.	I haven't done anything, I have done nothing.
Nous ne connaissons personne.	We don't know anyone.

The French negative pronouns are:

ne ... aucun(e) (de)	none (of), not any (of)
ne ... nul(le)	no one
ne ... pas un(e) (de)	not one (of)
ne ... pas un(e) seul(e) (de)	not a single one (of)
ne ... personne	no one

ne . . . rien	nothing, not . . . anything

Negative pronouns can be the subject, direct object, or indirect object of a sentence.

Rien n'a été fait.	Nothing was done.
Je n'ai rien fait.	I didn't do anything.
Je ne pense à personne.	I'm not thinking about anyone.

Alert!

The negative pronouns *ne . . . aucun*, *ne . . . pas un*, and *ne . . . pas un seul* must always have an antecedent. *Aucun de mes amis n'est venu.* (None of my friends came.) *Mes amis ? Aucun n'est venu.* (My friends? None came.)

The negative conjunction *ne . . . ni . . . ni* means "neither . . . nor" and is used just like negative pronouns, with *ne* preceding the verb and each *ni* preceding one of the negated words.

Il n'est ni intelligent ni créatif.	He is neither intelligent nor creative.
Ni Jacques ni Luc ne sont venus.	Neither Jacques nor Luc came.

Exercices de contrôle

A. Make the following statements negative using the negative structure in parentheses.

1. *Je parle français. (ne pas)*

   _____

2. *Il a trouvé les livres. (ne jamais)*

   _____

3. *J'aime danser. (ne plus)*

_____

4. *Allez-vous étudier ? (ne pas)*

_____

5. *Aujourd'hui. (pas)*

_____

6. *Je sais. (informal pas)*

_____

7. *Il a fait. (ne rien)*

_____

8. *Qui va le faire ? (personne ne)*

_____

9. *J'ai une idée. (ne aucun)*

_____

10. *Nous connaissons un avocat. (ne pas un seul)*

_____

B. Respond to the following in complete sentences with yes (Y) or no (N). If the subject is *tu*, respond with *je*. If the subject is *vous*, respond with *nous*.

a. *Viens-tu ? (Y)*

_____

b. *Nage-t-il ? (N)*

_____

_____

c. *Est-ce que vous le savez ? (Y)*

_____

d. *Est-ce que David vient ? (N)*

_____

e. *Ne veux-tu pas manger ? (Y)*

_____

f. *Vous allez étudier, n'est-ce pas ? (N)*

_____

g. *Ils ne vont jamais finir ? (Y)*

_____

h. *N'avez-vous pas encore réussi ? (N)*

_____

i. *Tu ne connais pas un seul étudiant ?(Y)*

_____

j. *Pouvez-vous aller à la banque ? (N)*

_____

Chapter 13

Prepositions

A PREPOSITION IS a word or phrase used to indicate a relationship between a verb, adjective, or noun that precedes the preposition and a noun that follows the preposition. Some English prepositions are: about, above, to, below, with, before, after, around, at, and for. The French prepositions can be divided into categories including prepositions dealing with time and place, as well as those that are paired with verbs.

Introduction to Prepositions

Prepositions modify the action or state of being of the verb and its effect on the object of the preposition. Take the following example, in which the preposition meaning "to" illustrates the relationship between the verb ("talking") and the object, which is David.

Je parle à David.	I'm talking *to* David.
Il est de Montréal.	He is *from* Montreal.
Cette voiture est pour toi.	This car is *for* you.

Below are the most common French prepositions.

à	to, at, in
Je vais à Paris.	I'm going to Paris.
après	after
On mange après la fête.	We're eating after the party.

avant	before
Il est arrivé avant midi.	He arrived before noon.
avec	with
Tu viens avec nous ?	Are you coming with us?
chez	at the home/office of
Je vais chez Marie.	I'm going to Marie's house.
dans	in
Il est dans la boîte.	It's in the box.
de	from, of, about
Il est de Rouen.	He's from Rouen.
en	in, on, to
Elle est en prison.	She's in prison.
pour	for
C'est pour toi.	It's for you.
sans	without
Il dort sans oreiller.	He sleeps without a pillow.
sur	on
Le chat est sur la table.	The cat is on the table.
vers	toward
Marche vers la porte.	Walk toward the door.

 Fact

There is no simple translation for *chez* in English, as it has multiple meanings. *"Il est chez le médecin"* translates to: He's at the doctor's (office) and *C'est typique chez les enfants* is translated as: That's typical among/of children.

À and De

À and *de* are two of the most common French prepositions. In general, *à* means "to," "at," or "in," while *de* means "of" or "from." But these little words have other meanings and uses and often cause problems for French students because they don't always parallel English uses.

Places
À indicates a location or destination, while *de* precedes the starting point or origin.

Je vais à Cannes.	I'm going to Cannes.
Je pars d'Arles.	I'm leaving from Arles.

Distance
À indicates the distance, while *de* again indicates the starting point.

J'habite à deux kilomètres d'ici.	I live two kilometers from here.
C'est à 15 minutes de vous.	It's 15 minutes from you.

Possession
À is used in front of a name or stressed pronoun to emphasize the ownership of some item, while *de* + noun or name is the equivalent of the English possessive structure's.

un ami à moi	a friend of mine
l'ami de Paul	Paul's friend

Purpose Versus Contents
À indicates the purpose of the noun it modifies, while *de* indicates the contents.

un verre à vin	wine glass (glass for wine)
un verre de vin	glass of wine

Additional Uses of *à*
Further uses of the preposition *à* include:

1. Manner, style, or characteristic

fait à la machine	machine-made
à la mode	in fashion
une fille aux cheveux roux	red-haired girl

2. Measurement

acheter au gramme	to buy by the gram
payer à l'année	to pay by the year

3. Point in time

Il arrive à 10h00.	He arrives at 10:00.
Elle est morte à 79 ans.	She died at the age of 79.

Additional Uses of *de*

Further uses of the preposition *de* include:

1. Defining characteristic

le marché de l'immobilier	real estate market
une salle d'attente	waiting room
une classe de français	French class

2. Cause

mourir de soif	to die of / from thirst
mal de mer	seasick

3. Means/manner of doing something

rougir de honte	to blush with shame
parler d'une voix ferme	to speak firmly

 **Essential**

When followed by the definite articles *le* and *les*, *à* and *de* contract with them into a single word: *le* + *à* become *au*; *les* + *à* become *aux*; *le* + *de* become *du*; *les* + *de* become *des*.

Temporal Prepositions

The French prepositions for time can also be difficult for students, due to the many different French temporal prepositions: *à, en, dans, depuis, pendant, durant*, and *pour*. These prepositions are all used to indicate something related to time, but their usage rules are quite strict. Here is a summary of how these prepositions are used.

The preposition *à* indicates at what time something occurs:

Je me lève à 6h00.	I get up at 6:00.
Elle arrivera à minuit.	She will arrive at midnight.

En expresses the duration of an action or the month, season, or year in which it occurs:

J'ai fini en une heure.	I finished in an hour.
Elle va voyager en mars.	She's going to travel in March.

Dans indicates how much time before an action occurs:

Je vais partir dans une heure.	I'm going to leave in an hour.
Il arrivera dans une semaine.	He will arrive in one week.

 **Alert!**

Pour can only be used to express time in the future. When talking about the duration in the present or past, you must use *pendant* or *durant*.

Depuis indicates the duration of an action that is still going on in the present, or that was going on when something else occurred:

Il pleure depuis une heure.
He's been crying for an hour.

J'étudiais depuis cinq minutes quand il a téléphoné.
I'd been studying for five minutes when he called.

Pendant and *durant* indicate the total time of an action in the past, present, or future.

J'ai nettoyé pendant/durant une heure.
I cleaned for an hour.

Il peut danser durant/pendant cinq heures.
He can dance for five hours.

Pour is also used to indicate the duration of an event, but only in the future:

Je serai en France pour deux semaines.
I'll be in France for two weeks.

Geographical Prepositions

Because French prepositions do not always parallel English prepositions in terms of meaning and usage, and because French nouns are gendered, knowing which French preposition to use with countries, cities, and other geographical names can be somewhat confusing.

Geographical names like countries, states, and provinces, like all French nouns, have a gender. Which geographical preposition to use depends on the gender of the geographical word, thus knowing the gender of each geographical name is the key to prepositions. Most geographical names which end in *e* are feminine, while those that end in any other letter are masculine, though there are, of course, exceptions. In English, you use three different prepositions with geographical names, depending on where you are in relation to the place.

I'm going to France.
I'm in France.
I'm from France.

In French, the distinction between the first two examples is lost—whether you are "going to" a place or you "are in" a place, the same preposition is used: *Je vais en France, Je suis en France.* Thus in French there are only two prepositions to choose from for each type of geographical name. The difficulty lies in knowing which preposition to use for a city, a state and a country.

Countries and Continents

In French, nearly all countries that end in *e* are feminine and the rest are masculine. The following countries are masculine even though they end in e: *le Cambodge, le Mexique, le Mozambique, le Zaïre, le Zimbabwe.* All continents are feminine.

Masculine and plural countries, along with plural continents, take *à* (to, at) or *de* (from) plus the definite article. Feminine countries and continents take *en* (to, at) or *de* (from).

MASCULINE	FEMININE	PLURAL
au Maroc	en France	aux Fidji
à l'Iran	en Espagne	aux USA
du Maroc	de France	des Fidji
de l'Iran	d'Espagne	des USA

States and Provinces

Masculine states and provinces can be preceded by either *dans le* or *au* to mean to/in, and *du* to mean from unless they start with a vowel, in which case they take either *en* or *dans l'* (to/in), and *d'* or *de l'* (from). Feminine states take *en* to mean to/in and *de* to mean from.

MASCULINE	FEMININE
dans le Texas	*en Louisiane*
en Ohio	*en Alberta*
du Manitoba	*de Virginie*
d'Illinois	*de Géorgie*

 Alert!

The states of New York and Washington have slightly different rules, in order to distinguish between the cities and states by the same name. In addition to the preposition, the names of these two states must be preceded by *l'état de*: *dans/de l'état de New York*, *dans/de l'état de Washington*.

Cities and Islands

Unlike the other geographical names, the gender of an island or city does not affect which preposition must be used. The prepositions *à* and *de* (or *d'*) are used with cities and singular islands, while *aux* and *des* are used with plural islands.

CITY	SINGULAR ISLAND	PLURAL ISLANDS
J'habite à Londres.	*Je vais à Hawaï.*	*Je vais aux Fidji.*
Je suis de Rome.	*Je suis de Malte.*	*Je suis des Maldives.*

Verbs with Prepositions

Prepositions can be very different in French and English, and nowhere is this more evident than with verbs. In English, many verbs require a certain preposition in order for the meaning of the verb to be complete, such as "to look at" and "to take care of." The same is true in French, but the prepositions are often not the same as the ones required by their English counterparts—an element of French grammar that often stumps new students of the language.

The following list shows the preposition required after a number of common French verbs and expressions.

accepter de	to accept, agree to
aider à	to help to
apprendre à	to learn how to
arrêter de	to stop
arriver à	to manage / succeed in
assister à	to attend
s'attendre à	to expect to
avoir peur de	to be afraid of
cesser de	to stop, cease
choisir de	to choose to
se concentrer sur	to concentrate on
décider de	to decide to
demander à (quelqu'un)	to ask (someone)
donner quelque chose à quelqu'un	to give something to someone
douter de	to doubt
emprunter quelque chose à quelqu'un	to borrow something from someone
enseigner à	to teach to
entrer dans	to enter
envoyer (quelque chose) à (quelqu'un)	to send (something) to (someone)
essayer de	to try to
être à	to belong to
être pour	to be in favor of
s'excuser de	to apologize for
faire attention à	to pay attention to

finir de	to finish
goûter à (quelque chose)	to taste (something)
s'habituer à	to get used to
se hâter de	to hurry to
hésiter à	to hesitate to
s'intéresser à	to be interested in
inviter (quelqu'un) à	to invite (someone) to
se méfier de	to distrust, beware of
se moquer de	to make fun of
obéir à	to obey
s'occuper de	to be busy with
offrir de	to offer to
oublier de	to forget to
partir de	to leave
payer pour (quelqu'un)	to pay for (someone)
permettre à	to permit
persister à	to persist in
persuader de	to persuade to
se plaindre de	to complain about
plaire à	to please / be pleasing to
se presser de	to hurry to
promettre de (faire quelque chose)	to promise to (do something)
proposer de	to suggest
refuser de	to refuse to
regretter de	to regret
se rendre compte de	to realize
répondre à	to answer
résister à	to resist
ressembler à	to resemble
réussir à	to succeed in
rire de	to laugh at
songer à	to dream / think of
se souvenir de	to remember
téléphoner à quelqu'un	to call
tirer sur	to shoot at

traduire en (français)	to translate into (French)
travailler pour	to work for
venir de	to have just (done something)
vivre dans (la misère, la peur)	to live in (poverty, fear)
voyager en (train, taxi)	to travel by (train, taxi)

 Essential

The list of useful verbs with prepositions can be daunting, but with practice you will eventually know which preposition to use automatically. Practice by writing sentences using each verb and saying them out loud.

The meaning of some verbs changes depending on which preposition is used:

jouer à	to play (a game or a sport)
jouer de	to play (an instrument)
manquer à (quelqu'un)	to miss someone
manquer de	to neglect, fail to (do something); to lack
parler à	to talk to
parler de	to talk about
parler pour	to speak on behalf of
penser à	to think about (imagine)
penser de	to think about (opinion)
profiter à	to benefit / be profitable to
profiter de	to make the most of

réfléchir à	to consider
réfléchir sur	to think about, reflect upon

tenir à	to hold (something) to heart, to insist on
tenir de	to take after, resemble

A few verbs can take different prepositions but mean the same thing:

commencer à / de	to begin (to)
continuer à / de	to continue (to)
habiter (à)	to live at/in (preposition is optional)
rêver à / de	to dream of

The following French verbs are followed directly by an infinitive or direct object whereas their English counterparts require a preposition.

aller	to be going to
approuver	to approve of
attendre	to wait for
chercher	to look for
demander	to ask for
devoir	to have to, be obliged to
écouter (la radio)	to listen to (the radio)
envoyer chercher	to send for
essayer	to try on
être censé	to be supposed to
habiter	to live in
ignorer	to be unaware of
mettre	to put on
payer (le repas)	to pay for (the meal)
pleurer	to cry about
pouvoir	to be able to
prier	to pray to
puer	to stink of

regarder	to look at
réussir	to make a success of, to pull off
sentir	to smell of
soigner	to take care of
venir (dîner, aider)	to come (for dinner, to help)

Exercices de contrôle

A. Choose the correct preposition for the following phrases.

1. *Nous allons _____ la pharmacie.*

2. *C'est un livre _____ musique.*

3. *Je suis arrivée _____ Pierre.*

4. *Qu'est-ce qui est _____ la boîte ?* (in)

5. *Je vais _____ ma famille.* (with)

6. *Il étudie _____ deux heures.* (for)

7. *Elles ont étudié _____ deux heures.*

8. *On va partir _____ midi.* (at)

9. *Il va _____ Égypte.*

10. *Nous sommes _____ Milan.*

B. Which preposition, if any, needs to follow the following verbs?

a. *aider* _____

b. *entrer* _____

c. *oublier* _____

d. *penser* (to have an opinion) _____

e. *jouer* (to play a game) _____

      f. *continuer*   _____

      g. *chercher*   _____

      h. *commencer*   _____

      i. *écouter*   _____

      j. *venir* (to have just)   _____

Chapter 14

Objects and Adverbial Pronouns

OBJECTS AND ADVERBIAL PRONOUNS are small words that make a big difference. Learning about these important little French words can even improve your knowledge of English grammar, if you do not yet know what objects and adverbial pronouns are. While learning about French objects and adverbial pronouns can be useful for developing your English grammar skills, there are a few differences between the English and French uses of these words. Be aware of these differences and you will find that these helpful words are easy to master!

Direct Objects

The direct object is the person or thing that receives the action of the verb in a sentence. To find the direct object in a sentence, ask the question Who? or What? (Qui ? or Quoi ?)

> He sees Marie—*Il voit Marie.*
> Who does he see? Marie.
> I'm eating bread—*Je mange du pain.*
> What am I eating? Bread.

Both French and English have direct object pronouns which replace the direct object. This is so that we don't say things like "Marie was at the bank today. When I saw Marie I smiled." It's much more natural to say "Marie was at the bank today. When I saw *her* I smiled."

Fact

A verb that is followed by a direct object is a transitive verb, such as "to watch." A verb that does not require a direct object is an intransitive verb, such as "to sleep." Note that some verbs have both transitive and intransitive uses, such as "to eat."

There is at least one direct object pronoun for each grammatical person.

me / m'/ moi	me
te / t'	you
le / l'	him, it (masc)
la / l'	her, it (fem)
nous	us
vous	you
les	them

The biggest difference between French and English direct object pronouns is that in English, direct object pronouns follow the verb, but they precede the verb in French.

Je le mange.	I'm eating it.
Il la voit.	He sees her.
Je t'aime.	I love you.
Tu m'aimes.	You love me.

The only exception to the rule about placing the direct object pronoun before the verb is the affirmative imperative, where direct object pronouns follow the verb and are attached to it with hyphens. In addition, *me* changes to *moi.*

Regarde-moi.	Watch me.
Laissez-moi !	Leave me alone!
Amenons-le à la plage.	Let's take him to the beach.

Indirect Objects

Indirect objects differ from direct objects, which receive the action of the verb in the sentence. Indirect objects are the people or things in a sentence to/for whom/what the action of the verb occurs. They are often preceded by a preposition.

I'm talking to Marie—*Je parle à Marie.*
To whom am I talking?—To Marie.
He buys books for the school—*Il achète des livres pour l'école.*
For what does he buy books?—For the school.

Indirect object pronouns replace the indirect object. The French indirect object pronouns are:

me / m' / moi	me
te / t'	you
lui	him, her, it
nous	us
vous	you
leur	them

 Essential

Direct and indirect objects are not always the same in French and English. In the sentence *aidez-moi* (help me), *moi* is an indirect object (because *aider* requires the preposition *à*), whereas "me" is a direct object, because there is no preposition.

French indirect object pronouns, like direct object pronouns, must precede the verb:

Je lui parle.	I'm talking to *him*.
Il m'a acheté des livres.	He bought some books for *me*.
Je vous donne de l'argent.	I'm giving some money to *you*.
Elle m'a dit la vérité.	She told the truth to *me*.

Again, the above is true, except in the affirmative imperative.

Parle-moi.	Talk to me.
Donnez-lui un stylo.	Give him a pen.
Achetons-leur des livres.	Let's buy them some books.

If you're not sure whether something is a direct or indirect object, you can use the following general guideline: if the person or thing is preceded by a preposition, that person/thing is an indirect object. If it is not preceded by a preposition, it is usually a direct object. However, if there are two objects and no preposition, you may need to rewrite the sentence to find the preposition. For example: He gave me the book > He gave the book to me.

Adverbial Pronoun Y

The adverbial pronoun *y* is a small but very important word in French that is often found alongside direct and indirect objects. *Y* indicates a place that has already been mentioned and is normally translated by the word "there" in English. *Y* usually replaces a prepositional phrase beginning with a preposition like *à, chez, dans,* or *en.*

Tu vas au musée aujourd'hui ?	Are you going to the museum today?
Non, j'y vais demain.	No, I'm going (there) tomorrow.

Nous allons en France.	We're going to France.
Est-ce que tu y es allé ?	Have you gone there?

Il était chez le médecin.	He was at the doctor's office.
Il y était.	He was there.

Like direct and indirect object pronouns, *y* precedes the verb it modifies, except in the affirmative imperative.

Alert!

Note that "there" can often be omitted in English, but *y* can never be omitted in French. *Je vais* is not a complete sentence; you have to say *J'y vais*.

Y can also replace *à* + noun (except when the noun is a person, which would instead take the indirect object).

Je réponds à une lettre.	I'm responding to a letter.
J'y réponds.	I'm responding to it.
Penses-tu à notre idée ?	Are you thinking about our idea?
Y penses-tu ?	Are you thinking about it?
Tu dois réussir à l'examen.	You have to pass the test.
Tu dois y réussir.	You have to pass it.

Y is also found in the expression *il y a*, which means "there is" or "there are" (see Chapter 18 for explanation and usage of *il y a*).

Adverbial Pronoun *En*

En replaces *de* plus something, either the partitive article or *de* + indefinite article + noun. *En* is translated by "some," "any," or a number in English.

As-tu des idées ?	Do you have any ideas?
Oui, j'en ai.	Yes, I have some.
Il a envie d'un sandwich.	He wants a sandwich.
Il en a envie.	He wants one.
Je n'ai pas besoin d'argent.	I don't need any money.
Je n'en ai pas besoin.	I don't need any.
Va-t-en !	Go away!

Like direct object pronouns, indirect object pronouns, and the adverbial pronoun *y*, *en* precedes the verb it modifies, except in the affirmative imperative.

If there is a modifier like *beaucoup de* or a number in the sentence, *en* replaces the noun, and the modifier or number is placed at the end of the sentence.

Il a beaucoup de livres.	He has a lot of books.
Il en a beaucoup.	He has a lot (of them).
Je voudrais trois concombres.	I'd like three cucumbers.
J'en voudrais trois.	I'd like three (of them).
Nous avons besoin de vingt stylos.	We need twenty pens.
Nous en avons besoin de vingt.	We need twenty (of them).

Indefinite and negative pronouns that express a quantity are often used with *en*. (Remember that *en* is also a preposition. See Chapter 13 for examples of its usage.)

The indefinite pronouns *un autre, d'autres, certain, plusieurs,* and *quelques-uns* must be preceded by the pronoun *en* when they are the object of the verb, and the noun is dropped.

J'ai vu plusieurs étudiants.	I saw several students.
J'en ai vu plusieurs.	I saw several of them.
As-tu les livres ?	Do you have the books?
J'en ai quelques-uns.	I have some of them.

When the negative pronouns *ne . . . aucun, ne . . . pas un,* and *ne . . . pas un seul* are the direct object of the sentence, *en* must be used.

Mes amis ?	My friends?
Je n'en ai vu pas un seul.	I didn't see a single one (of them).
As-tu des idées ?	Do you have any ideas?
Non, je n'en ai aucune.	No, I don't have any.

Double Object Pronouns

Now that you understand direct object pronouns, indirect object pronouns, adverbial pronouns, and reflexive pronouns, your next challenge is to understand their word order when used together.

All of these pronouns precede whatever verb they modify, except when the verb is in the affirmative imperative. The potential difficulty arises when you need two of them in the same sentence and you need to figure out the order in which you should place them. The table below illustrates the order of priority for double object pronouns in a sentence.

Order for Double Object Pronouns

FIRST	SECOND	THIRD	FOURTH
me			
te	*le*	*lui*	
se	*la*	*y*	*en*
nous	*les*	*leur*	
vous			

 Essential

You may have noticed that *me*, for example, is a direct, indirect, and reflexive pronoun. *Me* comes first no matter which type of pronoun it is. The same is true for *te*, *nous*, etc.

Ne me les montre pas.	Don't show them to me.
Il nous en a donné.	He gave us some.
Ils nous l'ont dit.	They told it to us.

In the affirmative imperative, there are two differences: the pronouns follow the verb (attached by hyphens) and the order of the pronouns is a bit different.

le	*moi*	*nous*		
la	*toi*	*vous*	*y*	*en*
les	*lui*	*leur*		

The main differences are that the direct objects *le*, *la*, and *les* come first and *me* and *te* change the stressed pronouns *moi* and *toi*, respectively.

Donne-le-moi.	Give it to me.
Montrez-nous-en.	Show us some.

Cherche-le-moi.	Find it for me.
Emmène-nous-y.	Take us there.

Exercices de contrôle

A. Rewrite the following sentences with the correct object or adverbial pronoun.

1. *Je cherche mon chien.*

   _____

2. *Il veut les livres.*

   _____

3. *Nous avons écrit à Luc.*

   _____

4. *Je vais parler aux étudiants.*

   _____

5. *As-tu vu le film ?*

   _____

6. *Ils ne vont pas à la plage.*

   _____

7. *Avez-vous beaucoup d'idées ?*

   _____

8. *Allez au musée.*

   _____

9. *Cherchons ses clés.*

   _____

10. *Écoutez la radio.*

    _____

B. Rewrite the following sentences with the two pronouns, paying particular attention to word order.

a. *Il achète les vêtements pour les enfants.*

_____

b. *Nous irons chercher la clé chez Claudia.*

_____

c. *Je vais donner l'argent à la police.*

_____

d. *Elle ne veut pas étudier le français en France.*

_____

e. *J'ai trouvé des disques pour Ana.*

_____

f. *Achetez des livres à New York.*

_____

g. *Ne mange pas de biscuits dans la bibliothèque.*

_____

h. *Mettons la lettre sur la table.*

_____

i. *Donnez l'argent à votre père.*

_____

j. *Montre tes devoirs à tes amis.*

_____

Chapter 15

Clauses and Conjunctions

CLAUSES AND CONJUNCTIONS might sound a little daunting but in fact you probably use them every day without even knowing what they are! A clause is a group of words containing a subject and a verb and a conjunction is a word that links words or groups of words together.

Introduction to Clauses

Although a clause contains a subject and a verb, a clause is not the same thing as a sentence. A sentence must contain at least one clause, but a clause is not necessarily a sentence by itself – it can be a sentence fragment. There are three different kinds of clauses.

1. An independent clause expresses a complete idea and stands alone. It is neither dependent upon nor the dependent of another clause.

   J'ai dit la vérité.   I told the truth.
   L'homme habite ici.   The man lives here.

2. A main clause expresses something that is modified by one or more subordinate clauses.

   J'ai dit que tu avais tort.   I said that you were wrong.
   L'homme dont je parle   The man that I'm talking about
      habite ici.   lives here.

3. A subordinate or dependent clause does not express a complete idea and cannot stand alone: it is attached to a main clause by a subordinate conjunction or a relative pronoun. When introduced by a relative pronoun, it may be known as a relative clause.

J'ai dit que tu avais tort.	I said that you were wrong.
L'homme dont je parle	The man that I'm talking about
habite ici.	lives here.

Si Clauses

A *si* clause, also known as an "if . . . then" clause, a conditional, or a conditional sentence, is a particular type of grammatical structure that includes an "if" clause and a "then" clause and expresses an action that is or was dependent on another action or state of being. There are three main types of *si* clauses.

First Conditional

The first conditional expresses likely situations and has three possible constructions. In each of them, *si* (if) is followed by the present tense and indicates the condition. The tense that expresses the "then" varies.

Present—Present

This construction is used for things that happen regularly.

S'il pleut, il ne nage pas.	If it rains, (then) he doesn't swim.
Il ne nage pas s'il pleut.	He doesn't swim out if it rains.

Si je ne veux pas travailler, je regarde la télé.
If I don't want to work (then) I watch TV.
Je regarde la télé si je ne veux pas travailler.
I watch TV if I don't want to work.

Present—Future

This construction is used when an event is likely to occur. The present tense indicates the situation that is required before the other action will occur.

Si j'ai de l'argent, je l'achèterai.	If I have money, (then) I will buy it.
Je l'achèterai si j'ai de l'argent.	I will buy it if I have money.

Si tu essaies, tu réussiras.	If you try, (then) you will succeed.
Tu réussiras si tu essaies.	You will succeed if you try.

Present—Imperative

The present-imperative construction gives an order that is dependent on some condition. The present tense indicates the situation that is required before the other action can become a command.

Si tu veux, viens m'aider.
If you want to, (then) come help me.
Viens m'aider si tu veux.
Come help me if you want to. (If you don't want to, then don't worry about it.)

Si vous avez de l'argent, faites les courses.
If you have money, (then) go shopping.
Faites les courses si vous avez de l'argent.
Go shopping if you have money. (If you don't have money, someone else will take care of it.)

Second Conditional

The second conditional expresses unlikely situations—something that is contrary to reality or unlikely to occur. The imperfect follows *si*; it is the condition that must be met before the conditional action in the result clause can take place.

Si j'avais de l'argent, je l'achèterais.
If I had money, (then) I would buy it.
Je l'achèterais si j'avais de l'argent.
I would by it if I had money.
Reality: I don't have any money, but if I did (contrary to reality), I would buy it.

Si tu essayais, tu réussirais.
If you tried, (then) you would succeed.
Tu réussirais si tu essayais.
You would succeed if you tried.
Reality: You don't try, but if you did (unlikely to occur), you would succeed.

Third Conditional

The third conditional expresses hypothetical situations that are contrary to past fact and are therefore impossible. *Si* introduces the event in the pluperfect that would have had to be different in order for the event in the conditional perfect to have been possible.

Si j'avais eu de l'argent, je l'aurais acheté.
If I had had money, (then) I would have bought it.
Je l'aurais acheté si j'avais eu de l'argent.
I would have bought it if I had had money.
Reality: I didn't have money so I didn't buy it.

Si tu avais essayé, tu aurais réussi.
If you had tried, (then) you would have succeeded.
Tu aurais réussi si tu avais essayé.
You would have succeeded if you had tried.
Reality: You didn't try so you didn't succeed.

Si je vous avais vu, je vous aurais aidé.
If I had seen you, (then) I would have helped you.
Je vous aurais aidé si je vous avais vu.
I would have helped you if I had seen you.
Reality: I didn't see you so I didn't help you.

 **Essential**

> While *si* clauses can seem somewhat challenging to master, their most difficult aspect is remembering which verb tenses go together. If you train yourself through practice to match the *si* clause with the correct verb tenses, you will eventually incorporate *si* clauses seamlessly into your French speech.

In the following chart, the first verb tense listed is the one that follows *si* (if), and the second tense is the result clause—the event that is dependent on the first clause. All you have to do is memorize the verb tense pairs and you're all set.

1st conditional	likely situations	present	present, future, or imperative
2nd conditional	unlikely situations	imperfect	conditional
3rd conditional	impossible situations	pluperfect	conditional perfect

What is a Conjunction?

As mentioned previously, a conjunction links words or groups of words. There are two types of French conjunctions: coordinating conjunctions and subordinating conjunctions. The difference between coordinating and subordinating conjunctions is very simple: coordinating conjunctions join two words or groups of words with an equal value, while subordinating conjunction join a subordinate/dependent clause to a main clause.

1. Coordinating conjunctions join words and clauses.

   Il ne mange ni poulet ni poisson.
   He eats neither chicken nor fish.

Veux-tu aller en Irlande ou *en Égypte ?*
Do you want to go to Ireland or Egypt?

J'aime lire et *écrire.*
I like reading and writing.

Je veux essayer, mais *j'ai peur.*
I want to try, but I'm afraid.

In each example, the coordinating conjunction is joining similar things:

- *Poulet* and *poisson* are both foods
- *Irlande* and *Égypte* are both places
- *Lire* and *écrire* are both verbs
- *Je veux essayer* and *j'ai peur* are both independent clauses.

The most common coordinating conjunctions are:

car	because (since)
donc	so
et	and
et . . . et	both . . . and
ou	or
ne . . . ni . . . ni	neither . . . nor
mais	but

2. Subordinating conjunctions join dependent clauses to main clauses.

J'ai dit que *je suis américain.*
I said that I am American.

Il est parti parce qu'*il est en retard.*
He left because he is late.

Il travaille pour que *vous puissiez voyager.*
He works so that you can travel.

J'ai pleuré bien que *j'étais heureux.*
I cried even though I was happy.

The most common subordinating conjunctions are:

afin que	so that
ainsi que	just as, so as
alors que	while, whereas
à moins que	unless
après que	after, when
avant que	before
bien que	although
jusqu'à ce que	until
lorsque	when
parce que	because
pendant que	while
pour que	so that
puisque	since, as
quand	when
que	that
quoique	even though
quoi que	whatever, no matter what
sans que	without
tandis que	while, whereas

Relative Pronouns

Relative pronouns link subordinate clauses to main clauses, and the most important French relative pronouns are *qui* and *que*. There are no standard translations for these words; depending on context, the English equivalent might be "who," "whom," "that," or "which." Note that in French, relative pronouns are required, while in English, they are often optional.

Qui replaces the subject (person or thing) in the subordinate clause

> *Je cherche l'étudiant. Il a perdu son sac à dos. > Je cherche l'étudiant qui a perdu son sac à dos.*
> I'm looking for the student who lost his backpack.

> *Trouvez le chien. Il habite dans cette maison. > Trouvez le chien qui habite dans cette maison.*
> Find the dog that lives in this house.

Qui also replaces an indirect object (person only) after a preposition.

> *C'est l'homme avec qui j'habite.*
> That's the man with whom I live / That's the man I live with.

> *Le garçon à qui j'ai parlé est très intelligent.*
> The boy to whom I spoke / The boy (that) I spoke to is very smart.

> *La femme à côté de qui je me suis assis...*
> The woman next to whom I sat... / The woman (that) I sat next to...

Que replaces the direct object (person or thing)

> *J'ai acheté le livre. Mon frère l'aimait. > J'ai acheté le livre que mon frère aimait.*
> I bought the book (that) my brother liked.

Qui est le professeur ? Je l'ai vu aujourd'hui. > Qui est le professeur que j'ai vu aujourd'hui ?
Who is the teacher (that) I saw today?

The third relative pronoun, *lequel*, replaces an indirect object that is not a person.

Le livre *dans lequel* j'ai vu ...
The book *in which* I saw ...

La ville *à laquelle* je songe ...
The town *about which* I'm dreaming ...

Le parc *près duquel* j'ai mangé ...
The park *near which* I ate / The park I ate near ...

Indefinite Relative Pronouns

Indefinite relative pronouns are similar in usage to relative pronouns: they link subordinate/relative clauses to main clauses. The difference is that regular relative pronouns have a specific antecedent, while indefinite relative pronouns do not.

There are four common indefinite relative pronouns; each form is used only in a particular structure, as summarized in the following table.

USAGE	PRONOUN	MEANING
Subject	*ce qui*	what
Direct object	*ce que/qu'*	what
Object of *de*	*ce dont*	which, what
Object of another preposition	*quoi*	which, what

 *Fact*

Remember that *que*, *qui*, and *lequel* are also interrogative pronouns and that *lequel* contracts with the prepositions *à* and *de*, and that the pronoun *tout* can be used with indefinite relative pronouns, and changes the meaning to "everything" or "all."

Ce qui serves as the subject of a relative clause and takes the *il* form of the verb.

Ce qui m'attire, c'est la couleur.	What attracts me is color.
Sais-tu ce qui l'intéresse ?	Do you know what interests him (or her)?
C'est ce qui m'énerve.	That's what annoys me.
Tout ce qui brille n'est pas or.	All that glitters is not gold.

Ce que is used as the indefinite direct object in a relative clause.

Ce que je veux, c'est une voiture.	What I want is a car.
Sais-tu ce que Luc a vu ?	Do you know what Luc saw?
C'est ce que j'aime.	That's what I love.
Tout ce qu'il dit est intéressant.	Everything he says is interesting.

Ce dont is used as the object of the preposition *de*.

Ce dont j'ai envie, c'est un chat.	What I want is a cat.
Sais-tu ce dont Jacques parle ?	Do you know what Jacques is talking about?
Ce n'est pas ce dont je me souviens.	That's not what I remember.
Je cherche tout ce dont j'ai besoin.	I'm looking for everything I need.

Quoi is the object of any other preposition.

Sais-tu à quoi je pense ?
Do you know what I'm thinking about?

J'ai travaillé, après quoi je suis allé au parc.
I worked, after which I went to the park.

Avec quoi écris-tu ?
What are you writing with?

 Alert!

French verbs often require different prepositions than English verbs, so you really need to be careful with *ce dont* and *quoi*. When there is no preposition in French (regardless of whether there is one in English), you would use *ce que* rather than *"ce dont."*

When *à quoi* is found at the beginning of a clause or after *c'est*, the word *ce* must be placed in front of it (*ce à quoi*).

Ce à quoi je m'attends, c'est une invitation.
What I'm waiting for is an invitation.

C'est ce à quoi Brigitte rêve.
That's what Brigitte dreams about.

Exercices de contrôle

A. Find the conjunction or relative pronoun in each of the following sentences and identify it as a coordinating conjunction, subordinating conjunction, relative pronoun, or indefinite relative pronoun.

1. *Je pense que le français est facile.*

   _____

2. *Jacques et Nicolas viennent à midi.*

   _____

3. *Voici ce que j'ai trouvé.*

_____

4. *Préfères-tu faire la lessive ou bien aller au supermarché ?*

_____

5. *On doit rappeler parce que c'est urgent.*

_____

6. *Connais-tu la femme qui habite ici ?*

_____

7. *Le film auquel je pense a été tourné au Maroc.*

_____

8. *J'ai nettoyé la cuisine tandis que Chantal a fait les achats.*

_____

9. *Soit Lise soit Marie va nous aider.*

_____

10. *Il a tout ce dont il a besoin.*

_____

B. Conjugate the verbs into the appropriate tenses/moods for the *si* clause type in parentheses.

a. *Si tu ne (être) pas fatigué, (raconter) moi une histoire.* (first conditional, type 3)

_____

b. *Il (chanter) toute la journée s'il (être) heureux.* (first conditional, type 1)

_____

c. *Si je (être) riche, je (acheter) une voiture.* (second conditional)

_____

d. *Est-ce que nous (voir) s'il (tomber)?* (first conditional, type 2)

_____

e. *Si elle me (donner) de l'argent, je (voyager).* (second conditional)

_____

f. *Il ne (pouvoir) pas dormir s'il (faire) chaud.* (second conditional)

_____

g. *S'ils (être) prêts, nous (partir).* (third conditional)

_____

h. *Sa mère (téléphoner) si Michel (être) malade.* (second conditional)

_____

i. *Si tu (vouloir) étudier, tu (devoir) le leur dire.* (third conditional)

_____

j. *Ils me (dire) s'ils (vouloir) venir.* (third conditional)

_____

Chapter 16

Adverbs

ADVERBS, LIKE ADJECTIVES, are not a required part of a sentence. Compare "I went home" to "I immediately went home." The second sentence is more precise, but the first is still logical and grammatically correct. That's not to say that adverbs are not important—on the contrary, they can add considerable detail to a statement. There are different types of adverbs, including adverbs of frequency, time, place, quantity, and adverbs of manner.

Introduction to Adverbs

An adverb is an invariable word that modifies a verb, an adjective, or another adverb. Adverbs provide details like when, how, where, how often, or to what degree something is done about the word they modify. There are many different types of French adverbs.

Adverbs of frequency
Adverbs of frequency explain how often something happens.

encore	again
encore une fois	one more time, once again
jamais	ever, never
parfois	sometimes
rarement	rarely
souvent	often
toujours	always, still

quelquefois	sometimes
tous les jours (mois, etc.)	every day (month, etc.)
une (deux, trois) fois	once (twice, three times)

 Question?

How can *jamais* mean both ever and never?
When used with *ne*, it means never. When used without *ne*, it means ever. Compare: *As-tu jamais voyagé ?* (Have you ever traveled?) *Non, je n'ai jamais voyagé.* (No, I have never traveled.)

Adverbs of Place

Adverbs of place indicate where something happens.

ailleurs	elsewhere
autour	around
d'ailleurs	besides
dedans	inside
dehors	outside
derrière	behind
dessous	below
dessus	above
devant	in front
en bas	down(stairs)
en haut	up(stairs)
ici	here
là	there
là-bas	over there
loin	far away
n'importe où	anywhere
nulle part	nowhere
partout	everywhere
près	near
quelque part	somewhere

Adverbs of Time

French adverbs of time indicate when something occurs.

actuellement	currently
alors	then
après	after
aujourd'hui	today
aussitôt	as soon as
autrefois	formerly, in the past
avant	before
bientôt	soon
d'abord	first, at first
déjà	already, ever
demain	tomorrow
depuis	since
dernièrement	lately
enfin	at last, finally
ensuite	next
hier	yesterday
immédiatement	immediately
longtemps	for a long time
maintenant	now
n'importe quand	anytime
récemment	recently
tard	late
tôt	early
tout à l'heure	a little while ago, in a little while
tout de suite	right away

 *Alert!*

Note that *actuellement* and "actually" are false cognates. *Actuellement* means "currently"; the French translation of "actually" is *en fait*, which means "in fact."

Other Types of Adverbs

Other types of adverbs include interrogative and negative adverbs (which were discussed in Chapters 11 and 12, respectively) and adverbs of manner, adverbs of quantity, and comparative/superlative adverbs, which follow.

Adverbs of Manner

Adverbs of manner indicate how something happens. Most adverbs of manner end in *-ment*, which is equivalent to the English adverb ending, -ly. These adverbs are formed from French adjectives, as follows:

If the French adjective ends in a vowel, add *-ment* to form the adverb.

ADJECTIVE	FRENCH ADVERB	ENGLISH TRANSLATION
absolu	*absolument*	absolutely
poli	*poliment*	politely
vrai	*vraiment*	truly

If the French adjective ends in a consonant, add *-ment* to the feminine form.

MASCULINE ADJECTIVE	FEMININE	FRENCH ADVERB	ENGLISH TRANSLATION
franc	*franche*	*franchement*	frankly
sérieux	*sérieuse*	*sérieusement*	seriously
lent	*lente*	*lentement*	slowly

If the French adjective ends in *-ant* or *-ent*, remove the ending and add *-amment* or *-emment*.

ADJECTIVE	FRENCH ADVERB	ENGLISH TRANSLATION
apparent	*apparemment*	apparently
constant	*constamment*	constantly
suffisant	*suffisamment*	sufficiently

Essential

Nearly every French word that ends in *-ment* is an adverb, usually of manner. You can think of *–ment* in French as nearly always equivalent to *–ly* in English.

There are a few French adverbs of manner that don't end in *-ment*:

ainsi	thus
bien	well
debout	standing up
exprès	on purpose
mal	poorly, badly
mieux	better
pire	worse
vite	quickly
volontiers	gladly

Adverbs of Quantity

French adverbs of quantity explain how many or how much and are often followed by *de* + noun.

assez (de)	quite, fairly, enough
autant (de)	as much, as many
beaucoup (de)	a lot, many
bien de	quite a few
combien (de)	how many, much
encore de	more
moins (de)	less, fewer
pas mal de	quite a few
(un) peu (de)	few, little, not very
la plupart de	most

plus (de)	more
tant (de)	so much, so many
très	very
trop (de)	too much, too many

 **Alert!**

Bien de, encore de, and *la plupart de* are always followed by the definite article and *très* is the only adverb of quantity that is never followed by *de* + noun; it can only be followed by an adjective or another adverb.

Adverbs of quantity can follow a verb, be followed by an adjective or adverb, or followed by *de* + noun. In the latter construction, the noun usually does not have an article in front of it.

C'est plus intéressant.	That's more interesting.
Je n'ai pas assez dormi.	I didn't sleep enough.
Il y a beaucoup de problèmes.	There are a lot of problems.
J'ai moins d'amis que mon frère.	I have fewer friends than my brother.

However, when the noun after *de* refers to specific people or things, the definite article is used and contracts with *de* just as the partitive article would. Compare the following sentences to the above examples:

Beaucoup des problèmes sont graves.
A lot of the problems are serious.

These are specific problems, not problems in general.

Peu des amis de mon frère sont ici.
Few of my brother's friends are here.

This is a specific group of friends, not friends in general.

Comparatives and Superlatives

Comparatives and superlatives are the types of adverbs that compare adjectives, adverbs, verbs, and nouns.

Comparatives

There are three types of comparatives:

Superiority	plus ... que	more ... than or _____ er than
Inferiority	moins ... que	less ... than
Equality	aussi ... que	as ... as
Equality	autant que	as much/many as

Comparisons with *plus* and *moins* can be made with adjectives, adverbs, nouns, and verbs. *Aussi que* is used with adjectives and adverbs, while *autant que* is used with nouns and verbs.

Je suis plus sportif (qu'Anne).	I'm more athletic (than Anne).
Nice est moins urbain (que Paris).	Nice is less urban (than Paris).
Tu es aussi grand que Michel.	You're as tall as Michel.
J'étudie autant que toi.	I study as much as you do.

For each part of speech, the comparison can be made with another person/thing (noun or pronoun) or with another of the same part of speech.

Adjectives

David est plus grand que Jacques.	David is taller than Jacques.
David est moins fier que Jacques.	David is less proud than Jacques.
David est aussi riche que travailleur.	David is as rich as (he is) hard-working.

Adverbs

David lit plus lentement que Jacques.	David reads more slowly than Jacques.
David écrit moins souvent que Jacques.	David writes less often than Jacques.
David travaille aussi vite que joyeusement.	David works as quickly as (he does) cheerfully.

Nouns

David a plus de livres que Jacques.	David has more books than Jacques.
David veut avoir autant d'amis que Jacques.	David wants as many friends as Jacques.
David a moins de livres que de jouets.	David has fewer books than toys.

Verbs

David travaille plus que Jacques.	David works more than Jacques.
David a étudié autant que Jacques.	David studied as much as Jacques.
David rit autant qu'il pleure.	David laughs as much as he cries.

Superlatives

Superlatives express the best, most, worst, and least. The superlative is formed with the definite article + *plus* or *moins* + adjective or adverb. With adjectives that normally follow the noun they modify (see Chapter 3) as well as with all adverbs, the superlative construction follows the noun. With adjectives that normally precede the noun, you can place the superlative either before or after the noun.

Sophie est la personne la plus intelligente que je connais.
Sophie is the most intelligent person that I know.

Marc est le garçon le plus sportif de l'école.
Marc is the most athletic boy in school.

Paris et Londres sont les villes les plus intéressantes du monde.
Paris and London are the most interesting cities in the world.

J'ai acheté le plus joli chiot./ J'ai acheté le chiot le plus joli.
I bought the prettiest puppy.

Est-il le plus jeune salarié ?/ Est-il le salarié le plus jeune ?
Is he the youngest employee?

When the superlative follows the noun, the sentence has two definite articles.

Bon, Vien, Mauvais

Bon, *bien*, and *mauvais* are exceptions to the above rules. *Bon* and *bien* have irregular forms for the comparative and superlative, while *mauvais* has both regular and irregular forms.

	COMPARATIVE	SUPERLATIVE
Bon(ne)	meilleur(e)	le/la meilleur(e)
Bien	mieux	le/la mieux
Mauvais(e)	pire	le/la plus mauvais(e)
	plus mauvais(e)	le/la pire

In the comparative, *meilleur, mieux, pire*, and *plus mauvais* precede the word they modify. In the superlative, when modifying a noun, *meilleur, pire*, and *plus mauvais* precede the noun. When modifying a verb, *mieux* and *pire* are placed after the verb.

Les tapis sont meilleurs que la moquette.
Rugs are better than carpet.

Elle est la meilleure étudiante de l'école.
She's the best student in the school.

Il parle mieux que toi.
He speaks better than you.

Je parle le mieux.
I speak the best.

Mentir est pire que voler. / Mentir est plus mauvais que voler.
Lying is worse than stealing.

C'est le pire film que j'aie jamais vu. / C'est le plus mauvais film que j'aie jamais vu.
It's the worst movie I've ever seen.

Placement of Adverbs

Generally speaking, French adverbs are placed after the verb they modify. However, placement depends to some extent upon the type of adverb and the word that it is modifying. Short adverbs that modify a verb usually follow the conjugated verb.

Tu chantes bien.	You sing well.
Tu as bien chanté.	You sang well.
Tu vas bien chanter.	You will sing well.

Il fait toujours la vaisselle.	He always does the dishes.
Il a toujours fait la vaisselle.	He always did the dishes.
Il doit toujours faire la vaisselle.	He always has to do the dishes.

 Essential

In compound tenses and dual-verb constructions, the adverb follows the first (conjugated) verb, not the past participle or infinitive.

Adverbs of frequency are usually placed after the verb.

Je fais toujours mes devoirs.	I always do my homework.
Luc ne fait pas souvent ses devoirs.	Luc doesn't often do his homework.

Adverbs of time which refer to specific days can be placed at the beginning or end of the sentence.

Aujourd'hui, tu dois m'aider.	Today, you have to help me.
Je travaillerai demain.	I'll work tomorrow.

Long adverbs are usually placed at the beginning or end of the sentence.

Généralement, je mange à midi.	Normally, I eat at noon.
Je ne sais pas, malheureusement.	I don't know, unfortunately.

However, if the long adverb specifically modifies the verb, it is placed after the conjugated verb.

Il a immédiatement quitté Londres.	He left London immediately.

Adverbs of place are usually found after the direct object.

Il a mis tes clés là-bas.	He put your keys over there.
J'ai trouvé le livre ici, sur la table.	I found the book here, on the table.

Adverbs which modify adjectives or other adverbs are placed in front of the word they modify.

Tu es très jolie.	You're very pretty.
Mathieu fait assez souvent la lessive.	Mathieu does the laundry fairly often.

In negative constructions, adverbs which normally follow the verb are placed after *pas*.

Je nage bien > Je ne nage pas bien.
I swim well > I don't swim well.

Tu étudies trop > Tu n'étudies pas trop.
You study too much > You don't study too much.

Exercices de contrôle

A. Turn the following adjectives into adverbs.

1. *admirable* _____

2. *passionné* _____

3. *naturel* _____

4. *premier* _____

5. *vif* _____

6. *intelligent* _____

7. *bruyant* _____

8. *patient* _____

9. *confortable* _____

10. *spontané* _____

B. Translate the adverb in parentheses into French and place it in the following sentences, making any other necessary changes (for example, you may need to replace an adjective with a comparative adverb).

a. *Tu parles.* (a lot)

_____

b. *Il est sorti.* (already)

_____

c. *Je vais en France.* (rarely)

_____

d. *Il y a du bruit.* (too much)

_____

_____

e. *Les étudiants sont prêts.* (most of)

_____

f. *Thomas est grand et Pierre est grand.* (as tall)

_____

g. *Ce livre est intéressant.* (less interesting)

_____

h. *Lise est une fille intelligente.* (smartest)

_____

i. *Voici une bonne idée.* (better)

_____

Chapter 17

Agreement

AGREEMENT REFERS TO the correspondence of gender, number, and/or person between different parts of speech, such as a noun and the adjective that modifies it. Agreement is one of the most difficult aspects of the French language for non-native speakers and even some native speakers, as there are numerous different types of grammatical agreement and the rules are fairly complicated. This chapter will help you understand the basics of French agreement.

Agreement of Adjectives

As you learned in Chapter 3, all types of French adjectives (descriptive, indefinite, negative, etc.) normally have to agree in gender and number with the nouns that they modify.

Ces *films sont* bons.	These movies are good.
Ma petite *voiture* verte.	My little green car.

There are, however, three exceptions.

Invariable Adjectives
Some French adjectives are invariable, meaning that they do not change to agree in gender and number with the nouns they modify. Here are some of the most common ones:

UNCHANGING FRENCH ADJECTIVE	ENGLISH TRANSLATION
angora	angora
auburn	auburn
chic	chic, stylish
kaki	khaki
kascher	kosher
kitsch	kitsch
marron	chestnut brown
ocre	ochre
orange	orange
sexy	sexy
snob	snobbish
standard	standard
sympa	nice

 Fact

Invariable adjectives are usually either those that were borrowed from other languages and don't lend themselves well to the French rules of agreement, or those that are also nouns, such as *orange*, which is both a color and a fruit.

Compound Colors

When adjectives of color are modified by another adjective or a noun, both words are invariable.

une chemise bleu clair	light blue shirt
des chapeaux rouge foncé	dark red hats
des yeux bleu vert	blue-green eyes
la tasse vert pomme	apple green cup

When two adjectives of color are joined by *et* (and), they may or may not agree with the noun they modify.

une chemise bleu et vert   *une chemise bleue et verte*
des chapeaux rouge et noir   *des chapeaux rouges et noirs*

Adjectives Used as Adverbs

When French adjectives are used as adverbs (that is, they modify verbs rather than nouns), they are invariable.

bas	quietly
bon	good
cher	expensive
clair	clearly
court	short
droit	straight
dur	hard
fin	small, thin, finely
fort	loudly
franc	frankly
grand	big
haut	high
mauvais	bad
vieux	old

Note that the translations given here are for the adjectives that are used as adverbs. When these adjectives are used as adjectives, the meaning may be different. For example, *bas* means "low" as an adjective and "quietly" as an adverb.

Agreement of Pronouns

Pronouns come in two varieties: personal and impersonal. Personal pronouns change to agree in gender, number, and person with the grammatical person that they represent.

	SUBJECT	DIRECT OBJECT	INDIRECT OBJECT	REFLEXIVE	STRESSED
I	je	me	me	me	moi
you	tu	te	te	te	toi
he, it (m)	il	le	lui	se	lui
she, it (f)	elle	la	lui	se	elle
one	on			se	soi
we	nous	nous	nous	nous	nous
you	vous	vous	vous	vous	vous
they (m)	ils	les	leur	se	eux
they (f)	elles	les	leur	se	elles

Some impersonal pronouns change to agree in gender and number with the nouns they replace.

	MASCULINE SINGULAR	FEMININE SINGULAR	MASCULINE PLURAL	FEMININE PLURAL
Demonstrative	celui	celle	ceux	celles
Indefinites	un autre	une autre	d'autres	d'autres
	certain	certaine	certains	certaines
	chacun	chacune		
Interrogatives	lequel	laquelle	lesquels	lesquelles
Negatives	ne ... aucun	ne ... aucune		
	ne ... nul	ne ... nulle		
	ne ... pas un (seul)	ne ... pas une (seule)		
Possessives	le mien	la mienne	les miens	les miennes
	le nôtre	la nôtre	les nôtres	les nôtres

For a list of all of the possessive pronoun forms, see Chapter 19.

Être Verbs, and Passive Voice

In Chapter 9, you learned that compound verb tenses like the *passé composé* are conjugated with either *avoir* or *être*. When conjugating *être* verbs (*aller, sortir, venir,* etc.) in any of the compound tenses and moods, the past participle has to agree with the subject of the sentence in gender and number.

Elle est venue.	She came.
Nous étions arrivés.	We had arrived.
Elles sont parties.	They left.
Ils seront allés.	They will have gone.

 Alert!

When verbs with *être* are used transitively, they are conjugated with *avoir*. When this happens, they do not agree with the subject, but they may agree with the direct object.

To make the past participle agree, just add *e* for feminine and *s* for plural.

MASCULINE SINGULAR	FEMININE SINGULAR	MASCULINE PLURAL	FEMININE PLURAL
allé	*allée*	*allés*	*allées*
sorti	*sortie*	*sortis*	*sorties*
venu	*venue*	*venus*	*venues*

The passive voice is also conjugated with *être* plus the past participle, thus verbs conjugated in the passive voice must also agree in gender and number with their subject.

Les vêtements sont lavés par nos enfants.
The clothes are washed by our children.

Ma soeur est respectée de tous ses profs.
My sister is respected by all of her teachers.

Les exercices sont faits par les étudiants.
The exercises are done by the students.

Remember that the subject of the passive voice is not the person performing the action, but the person or object that the action is being performed on.

Agreement with Direct Objects

The majority of French verbs are conjugated with *avoir* as the auxiliary verb in the compound tenses. Unlike *être* verbs, which require agreement between the subject and past participle, *avoir* verbs do not require this type of agreement.

J'ai acheté une voiture.	I bought a car.
Il a reçu des livres.	He received some books.
Avez-vous vu mes soeurs ?	Have you seen my sisters?

However, verbs conjugated with *avoir* require a different type of agreement: when a direct object or direct object pronoun precedes the past participle, the past participle must agree with whatever the direct object is referring to.

Je l'ai achetée.	I bought it (the car).
Les livres qu'il a reçus...	The books he received...
Les avez-vous vues ?	Have you seen them (my sisters)?

When *être* verbs are conjugated with *avoir*, they too may require direct object agreement.

La voiture que j'ai sortie...	The car I took out...
Je les ai montés.	I took them up.

When the direct object follows the verb, there is no agreement. Agreement is needed only when the direct object precedes the verb. There is never agreement with an indirect object that precedes the verb.

Je leur ai acheté des livres.	I bought them some books.
Il nous a dit la vérité.	He told us the truth.
Elle m'a donné de l'argent.	She gave me some money.

Agreement with Pronominal Verbs

In compound tenses, pronominal verbs are conjugated with *être*. Like *être* verbs and the passive voice, the past participle of pronominal verbs normally has to agree with the subject of the sentence.

Lise et Chantal se sont levées.	Lise and Chantal got up.
Ils se seraient blessés si...	They would have injured themselves if...
Elle s'est couchée à minuit.	She went to bed at midnight.

However, this is only true when the reflexive pronoun is the direct object of the sentence; in other words, when the direct object and the subject are one and the same. When the reflexive pronoun is the indirect object, the past participle does not agree. In the examples below, the direct object is in bold. Because the direct object follows the verb, there is no agreement.

Ils se sont dit la vérité.	They told each other the truth.
Il s'est acheté des stylos.	He bought himself some pens.
Sylvie, tu t'es lavé les mains *?*	Sylvie, did you wash your hands?

If the direct object were to precede the verb, it would need to agree:

Ils se la sont dite.	They told it to each other.
Il se les est achetés.	He bought them for himself.
Sylvie, tu te les es lavées ?	Sylvie, did you wash them?

Note that for all verbal agreement—*être* verbs, direct object with *avoir* verbs, and pronominal verbs—agreement only occurs in the compound tenses. There is never any agreement in the simple tenses (present, future, conditional, imperfect). The only exception to this is in the passive voice, which is a compound conjugation even in the simple tenses.

Essential

When a sentence has two objects, the reflexive pronoun is always the indirect object and so the past participle does not agree with it.

For some verbs, the reflexive pronoun is always an indirect object, which means that the past participle will never change to agree with it. Most verbs that always have an indirect object reflexive pronoun are reciprocal: to ___ (to) one another.

s'acheter	to buy (for) oneself
se demander	to wonder
se dire	to say to each other, to tell oneself
se donner	to give each other, to give oneself
s'écrire	to write to each other
se faire mal	to hurt oneself
s'imaginer	to imagine, think
se parler	to talk to each other
se plaire (à faire . . .)	to enjoy (doing)

se promettre	to promise each other, to promise oneself
se rendre compte de	to realize
se rendre visite	to visit each other
se ressembler	to resemble each other
se rire (de quelqu'un)	to mock (someone)
se sourire	to smile at each other, to smile to oneself
se téléphoner	to call each other

Exercices de contrôle

A. Make the adjectives in the following sentences agree, if necessary.

1. *C'est une idée intéressant.*

   _____

2. *Elle est très chic.*

   _____

3. *À vous parler franc . . .*

   _____

4. *Préférez-vous la chemise vert ou la chemise bleu clair ?*

   _____

5. *J'ai vu deux films étranger la semaine passé.*

   _____

6. *Il porte des chaussures blanc et noir.*

   _____

7. *Je cherche une boucherie kascher.*

   _____

8. *Ils travaillent dur.*

   _____

9. *Elle a des cheveux auburn.*

_____

10. *Nous cherchons une ceinture vert foncé.*

_____

B. Make the following sentences agree as needed.

a. *Hélène s'est levé à huit heures.*

_____

b. *Nous sommes allé à la banque.*

_____

c. *Voici les clés qu'il a perdu.*

_____

d. *Elles sont sorti hier soir.*

_____

e. *Cette femme est très respecté.*

_____

f. *Les lampes que Lise a acheté ne marchent pas.*

_____

g. *Ils se sont réveillé trop tard.*

_____

h. *Où est la table que nous avons vu hier ?*

_____

i. *Les meubles seront refait jeudi.*

_____

j. *Élisabeth, t'es-tu lavé les mains ?*

_____

Chapter 18

Presentatives and Determiners

PRESENTATIVES AND DETERMINERS are two related categories of terms which introduce nouns while at the same time emphasizing or modifying them. Presentatives simultaneously introduce and emphasize something. Determiners, on the other hand, introduce and at the same time modify nouns. Both groups of words are helpful to know and help you avoid confusion when you are trying to understand fluent French speakers.

Introduction to Presentatives

While they are significant words that serve multiple functions, presentatives are not a part of speech so much as a small group of assorted terms used in this way, including prepositions, conjunctions, adverbs, and expressions.

à	to
À table !	(come) to the table!
à bas	down with
À bas le fascisme !	Down with fascism!
c'est, ce sont	this/it is, these are
C'est une bonne histoire.	It's a good story.
dire que	to think that
Dire qu'il aurait pu mourir !	To think that he could have died!
étant donné	given
Étant donné votre situation . . .	Given your situation . . .

il y a	there is/are
Il y a trois chaises.	There are three chairs.
soit, soient	let there be
Soit un triangle . . .	Let there be / Take a triangle
vive, vivent	long live
Vive la France !	Long live France!
voici	here is/are
Voici ma voiture.	Here is my car.
voilà	there is
Voilà la maison.	There's the house (over there).

C'est and *Il est*

C'est and *il est* are two of the most important French presentatives. They may be translated by this/that/it is, they are, or he/she is.

Votre village ? C'est très joli !	Your village? It's very pretty!
Il est difficile d'être honnête.	It's difficult to be honest.
Ana ? C'est une fille sympa.	Ana? She's a nice girl.
Il est tard.	It's late.

C'est and *il est* are the standard presentatives and are commonly used in impersonal expressions and general comments: It's possible, It's interesting, It's difficult, It's too bad, etc. However, *c'est* and *il est* have other forms that may be used when they are referring to specific nouns.

C'est normally becomes *ce sont* when followed by a plural noun.

Ce sont mes parents.	These are my parents.
Ce sont nous qui avons décidé.	It's us that decided.
Ce sont des étudiants ?	Are they students?

In informal French, *c'est* is often used with both singular and plural nouns: *C'est nous qui avons décidé. Il est* becomes *elle est, ils sont,* or *elles sont,* according to the gender and number of the noun that it is replacing or introducing.

Marie-Laure ? Elle est avocate.	Marie-Laure? She's a lawyer.
Ils sont en France.	They are in France.

Although the expressions *c'est* and *il est* have similar meanings, they cannot be used interchangeably. In fact, the rules for their usage are quite strict—the following table summarizes what each of them can be used with. *C'est* can be followed by:

A MODIFIED NOUN

C'est un avocat.	He's a lawyer.
C'est mon frère.	That's my brother.

AN ADJECTIVE

C'est bon.	It's good.
Ce n'est pas évident.	It's not easy.

A MODIFIED ADVERB

C'est trop tard.	It's very late.
C'est trop loin.	It is too far away.

A PROPER NAME

C'est Michel.	It's Michel.
Ce sont Laure et Marie.	It is Laure and Marie.

A STRESSED PRONOUN

C'est moi.	It's / That's me.
C'est lui qui veut y aller.	It's him that wants to go.

Il est can be used with the following:

AN UNMODIFIED NOUN

Il est avocat.	He's a lawyer.
Elle est actrice.	She's an actress.

AN ADJECTIVE (PERSON)

Il est sportif.	He is athletic.
Elle est belle.	She is beautiful.

AN UNMODIFIED ADVERB

Il est tard.	It's late.
Elles sont ici.	They are here.

A PREPOSITIONAL PHRASE

Il est en France.	He's in France.
Elle est à l'école	She is at school.

 Essential

The word "modified" refers to any sort of additional information given about a word. For example, in the sentence *C'est un avocat*, "avocat" is modified by the indefinite article *un*. In contrast, in *Il est avocat*, "avocat" is unmodified. Likewise for *C'est trop tard* (*tard* is modified by *trop*) versus *Il est tard* (*tard* is unmodified).

Il y a

Il y a is another extremely important French expression. *Il y a* means "there is" or "there are" and is usually followed by an indefinite article, adjective, or pronoun, or a number + noun.

Il y a un livre sur la table.	There's a book on the table.
Il y a des vêtements ici.	There are some clothes here.

Il y a plusieurs choses à faire.	There are several things to do.
Il y a quelque chose dans ton sac.	There's something in your bag.

It might help you to understand the three words that comprise the expression *il y a*:

1. *il*—the subject "it"
2. *y*—the pronoun "there"
3. *a*—the third person singular present tense of *avoir* (to have)

To make *il y a* negative, just place *n'* in front of *y* (because *ne* contracts to *n'* in front of *y* or a vowel) and place *pas* after *a*.

Il n'y a pas de livre sur la table.	There isn't any book on the table.
Il n'y a pas de vêtements ici.	There aren't any clothes here.

Remember that the indefinite article changes to *de* due to the negation.

To use *il y a* in another tense, you just conjugate *avoir* into that tense:

Il y avait un livre…	There was a book…
Il y aura un livre…	There will be a book…

You can ask a question with either use, *est-ce que* or inversion.

Est-ce qu'il y a un livre ?	Is there a book?
Est-ce qu'il y a des vêtements ?	Are there any clothes?

To invert *il y a*, start with the pronoun *y*, then invert *il* and *a*. This will give you two adjacent vowels (*a il*), so you will need to add a *t* surrounded with dashes between them (see Chapter 11):

Y a-t-il un livre ?	Is there a book?
Y a-t-il des vêtements ?	Are there any clothes?

You can also use *il y a* with interrogative words:

Pourquoi est-ce qu'il y a un livre sur la table ?   Why is there a book on the table?
Combien de livres y a-t-il ?   How many books are there?

 Alert!

Try not to confuse *il y a* with *depuis*. *Il y a* means "ago" while *depuis* means "for" or "since": *J'ai habité en France il y a cinq ans.* (I lived in France five years ago.) *J'habite en France depuis cinq ans.* (I have lived in France for five years.)

When *il y a* is followed by a period of time, it means "ago":

Je l'ai lu il y a deux semaines.   I read it two weeks ago.
Il y a un an que nous avons déménagé.   We moved a year ago.

Voici and Voilà

Voici and *voilà* mean "here is" and "there is," respectively. *Voici* and *voilà* are used when the speaker is actually handing something to another person, or pointing out to something or someone nearby.

Voici vos clés.   Here are your keys.
Voilà ton père.   There's your father (over there).

Question?

Voici and *voilà* are commonly preceded by the definite object or adverbial pronoun *en*.

Où est mon sac ? Le voilà.	Where is my bag? (It's) over there.
Tes livres ? Les voici.	Your books? Here they are.
Peux-tu me prêter de l'argent ?	Could you loan me some money?
En voilà.	Here you go.

In informal French, *voilà* is used considerably more often than *voici*—*voilà* tends to be used to mean both "here is" and "there is."

Voilà ton ami qui arrive.	Your friend is here.
Où est-il ? Le voilà.	Where is it? Here you go.

Voilà can also be used to respond to some kind of demand or question.

Voilà, j'arrive, j'arrive.	All right, I'm coming, I'm coming.
Voilà, j'ai terminé !	There, I'm done!
Et voilà !	That's it! That's all there is to it! So there you go!

Introduction to Determiners

Determiners introduce and at the same time modify nouns. Determiners include articles and certain types of adjectives; in fact, determiners are sometimes referred to as non-qualifying adjectives. Determiners are much more common in French than in English—nearly every noun in a French sentence must be preceded by some sort of determiner. Unlike qualifying (descriptive) adjectives, determiners always precede the noun they modify, cannot be modified, and cannot be used with other determiners. All articles are determiners.

ARTICLES	PURPOSE	FRENCH	ENGLISH
definite	refer to specific object	*le, la, les*	the
indefinite	refer to unspecified object	*un, une, des*	a, an, some
partitive	refer to unknown quantity	*du, de la, des*	some

 Fact

Determiners cannot be modified by other determiners, adjectives, or adverbs. However, they can be used with adjectives that modify the noun: *ma jeune fille* (my young daughter.)

Many types of adjectives are also determiners.

ADJECTIVES	PURPOSE	FRENCH	ENGLISH
demonstrative	indicate specific noun	*ce, cet, cette, ces*	this, that, these, those
exclamative	express strong sentiment	*quel(s), quelle(s)*	what a
indefinite	modify without specifying	*autre, certain ...*	other, certain ...
interrogative	ask "which?"	*quel(s), quelle(s)*	which
negative	negate or cast doubt	*ne ... aucun, nul*	no, not a single
possessive	indicate possessor	*mon, ton, son ...*	my, your, his ...

Exercices de contrôle

A. Fill in the blanks with the appropriate form of *c'est, il est,* elle est, etc.

1. *Le restaurant est fermé ? _____ difficile à croire.*

2. *Cet homme-là, _____ avocat.*

3. *_____ nous qui allons en France.*

4. *Ma soeur, _____ une artiste.*

5. *Ce musée, _____ très intéressant.*

6. *Voici David. _____ étudiant en histoire.*

7. *Qui est à la porte ? _____ Lise.*

8. *_____ actrice.*

9. *Je vois tes livres, _____ sur la table.*

10. *_____ mon ami qui l'a fait.*

B. Translate the following sentences into French using *il y a.*

a. There is a man in your office.

   _____

b. There were five students.

   _____

c. We saw her a week ago.

   _____

d. What's wrong?

   _____

e. How many tables are there?

   _____

f. There aren't any tables.

g. There will be a test tomorrow.

h. I ate an hour ago.

i. Is there any bread?

j. No, there's no bread.

Chapter 19

Possession

EXPRESSING POSSESSION in French is similar in many ways to English. Both languages have possessive adjectives and pronouns, and both have a third way to express possession using a name or noun. The biggest difference is that English has a total of three ways to express possession, but French has four. It is the fourth method of French possession that is the trickiest for students.

Possessive Adjectives

Possessive adjectives are the determiners used to indicate to whom or to what something belongs. French and English possessive adjectives are used similarly, but the French ones are a little more complicated when it comes to form: like most French adjectives, possessives have different forms for masculine and feminine, singular and plural.

ENGLISH	MASCULINE	FEMININE	BEFORE VOWEL	PLURAL
my	*mon*	*ma*	*mon*	*mes*
your (*tu* form)	*ton*	*ta*	*ton*	*tes*
his, her, its	*son*	*sa*	*son*	*ses*
our	*notre*	*notre*	*notre*	*nos*
your (*vous*)	*votre*	*votre*	*votre*	*vos*
their	*leur*	*leur*	*leur*	*leurs*

Keep in mind that when a feminine noun begins with a vowel, the masculine possessive is used instead of the feminine you might expect. This is done in order to avoid "hiatus"—the undesirable sound of two adjacent vowel sounds. Thus instead of *ma histoire*, where the flow of the sentence would be broken, you say *mon histoire*.

You can see that French has many more possessives than English, but they are not as complicated as you might think. Each singular grammatical person (I, you, he/she/it) has three forms of the possessive. The gender, number, and first letter of the noun being modified determine which form to use.

	MASCULINE	FEMININE	VOWEL	PLURAL
my	*mon stylo*	*ma montre*	*mon amie*	*mes frères*
your	*ton stylo*	*ta montre*	*ton amie*	*tes frères*
his, her, its	*son stylo*	*sa montre*	*son amie*	*ses frères*

For English native speakers, *the* most important thing to understand about possessive adjectives is that in French it is the gender of the noun that determines which form to use, not the gender of the subject. In English, "his book" and "her book" indicate that the first book belongs to a male and the second to a female. In French, on the other hand, both of those are translated by "son livre."

 Essential

If it is important to distinguish between his and her, you can add *à lui* or *à elle*:
C'est son livre à elle (It's *her* book).

Another important aspect of French possessive adjectives is that when you are describing two or more nouns, you must use a possessive adjective in front of each noun: his mother and father—*son père et sa mère*.

Plural subjects (we, you, they) have only two forms: singular and plural. The gender of the noun and the letter it begins with make no difference.

	MASCULINE	FEMININE	VOWEL	PLURAL
our	*notre livre*	*notre table*	*notre amie*	*nos tables*
your	*votre livre*	*votre table*	*votre amie*	*vos tables*
their	*leur livre*	*leur table*	*leur amie*	*leurs tables*

Possessive adjectives are never used with any type of article; in fact, they replace the article: *un livre*—a book, *mon livre*—my book.

Possessive *De*

The French preposition *de* is used to express possession with a noun or name. This is equivalent to 's or s' in English.

le livre de David	David's book
les musées de France	France's museums
les jouets de la fille	the girl's toys
les jouets des filles	the girls' toys

Note that the order of the nouns is inverted in French. France's museums translates literally as "the museums of France."

The possessor noun must be preceded by an article: the book's pages—*les pages du livre*, a book's pages—*les pages d'un livre*. As with the partitive article and other *de* constructions, *de* contracts with *le* and *les* to make *du* and *des*.

Possessive Pronouns

Possessive pronouns replace possessive adjectives plus nouns. Once again, French has different forms of the possessive pronoun depending on the gender and number of the noun it is replacing.

	SINGULAR		PLURAL	
	Masculine	*Feminine*	*Masculine*	*Feminine*
mine	*le mien*	*la mienne*	*les miens*	*les miennes*
yours (sing., fam.)	*le tien*	*la tienne*	*les tiens*	*les tiennes*
his/hers/its	*le sien*	*la sienne*	*les siens*	*les siennes*
ours	*le nôtre*	*la nôtre*	*les nôtres*	*les nôtres*
yours (plur., form.)	*le vôtre*	*la vôtre*	*les vôtres*	*les vôtres*
theirs	*le leur*	*la leur*	*les leurs*	*les leurs*

French and English possessive pronouns are very similar, with two exceptions: the French possessive pronoun must match the noun being replaced in number and gender, and a definite article must be used.

Voici mon mari.
Here's my husband.

Enchantée. Le mien est dans la cuisine.
Nice to meet you. Mine is in the kitchen.

J'aime bien ma classe, mais la tienne semble aussi intéressante.
I like my class, but yours seems interesting too.

Mes enfants sont en Italie. Où habitent les tiens ?
My kids are in Italy. Where do yours live?

Cet argent . . . c'est le tien ou le mien ?
This money . . . is it yours or mine?

 Fact

Similar to the possessive adjective, the third person possessive pronoun's form depends on the gender of the noun being replaced, not the gender of the subject. *Le sien, la sienne, les siens,* and *les siennes* can all mean his, hers, or its. *Le sien est ici* (His/Hers/Its is here.)

When the possessive pronoun is preceded by *à* or *de*, the preposition contracts with the definite article:

Tu penses à ta décision ; je dois penser à la mienne.
You think about your decision; I need to think about mine.

Ils parlent de leurs projets et nous parlons des nôtres.
They are talking about their plans and we are talking about ours.

Possessive *à*

The preposition *à* is used in French to express possession in a way that emphasizes the ownership of the object. It is this fourth type of French possession that is most difficult for French students, because it doesn't exist in English; it has to be translated by one of the other three methods.

The possessive *à* construction can be done with either *être* + *à* + stressed pronoun or name or *c'est* + noun + *à* + stressed pronoun or name.

Cet ordinateur est à lui.	This computer is his.
C'est une amie à Pierre.	She's a friend of Pierre's.
À qui est ce sac ?	Whose bag is this?
C'est à elle.	It's hers.
Cet argent... c'est à toi ou à moi ?	This money... is it yours or mine?
C'est à lui.	It's his.
Ce livre est à Chantal.	This is Chantal's book.
Non, c'est à moi !	No, it's mine!

Comparison of Possessives

All of these different possessive forms can seem a little confusing, so here is a summary to help you understand the differences between them and when to use each of them.

Possessive Adjectives

French possessive adjectives are used just like English possessive adjectives, to mean my, your, his, etc. They must be followed by a noun: *mon livre*—my book, *ses amis*—his/ her friends.

Possessive *de*

The possessive *de* is the French equivalent for name or noun + 's or s': *les amis de Marie*—Marie's friends, *les voitures des étudiants*—the students' cars. See the only exception to this in possessive *à*, below.

Possessive Pronouns

French possessive pronouns are generally used just like English possessive pronouns: *le mien est plus joli*—mine is prettier, *où sont les nôtres ?* where are ours? See the exception in possessive *à*, below.

Possessive *à*

The possessive *à* can be used only after the verb *être* or after *c'est* + noun. It emphasizes the ownership of the object, such as when you are trying to determine to whom something belongs: *c'est à moi ou à toi ?*—is it mine or yours? There are two types of constructions in which the possessive *à* replaces a different structure used in English.

1. **Possessive *à* replaces possessive *de***
   The only time 's or s' can be translated by something other than the possessive *de* is in the English construction noun + of + name, in which case the possessive *à* is used: *un ami à Marie*—a friend of Marie's (compare to *l'ami de Marie*—Marie's friend).
2. **Possessive *à* replaces possessive pronoun**
   To translate the English constructions noun + of + possessive pronoun and it is + possessive pronoun, French uses the possessive *à*: *un livre à moi*—a book of mine, *C'est à moi !* —It's mine!

Exercices de contrôle

A. Translate the following sentences into French using the possessive adjective or possessive *de*, as appropriate.

1. Here are my books.

   _____

2. Michel's father is a doctor.

   _____

3. I'm looking for your keys.

   _____

4. What is his favorite restaurant?

   _____

5. I don't like the teacher's ideas.

   _____

6. Their friends are very nice.

   _____

7. Students' cars must be locked.

   _____

8. Our house is over there.

   _____

9. She's my favorite actress.

   _____

10. There are my mother and my father.

    _____

B. Rewrite the following sentences with the possessive pronoun or possessive *à*, as appropriate. You may need to change verb forms and other grammatical structures. Note that some of them have more than one correct response.

a. *C'est mon livre.*

_____

b. *Voici nos clés.*

_____

c. *La voiture appartient à Marc.*

_____

d. *J'aime tes idées.*

_____

e. *Ce sont nos documents.*

_____

f. *Cet étudiant est dans la classe de Mme Lefèvre.*

_____

g. *Les livres sont pour Marc et Jean.*

_____

h. *C'est notre table ou votre table.*

_____

i. *Où est mon étudiante ?*

_____

j. *Leur classe est très petite.*

_____

Chapter 20

Writing in French

WRITING IN FRENCH can be a very different matter than speaking French, but a well-rounded language student should be able to do both. In addition, knowing how to write a word in French can very often help you better understand and remember its spoken form. By practicing writing in French, you may notice a similarity to the word's English counterpart, and the simple act of writing vocabulary helps you cement that word's meaning into memory.

Accents

There are five French accents: four for vowels and one for a consonant. These are not optional; in fact, an incorrect or missing accent is a spelling mistake just like an incorrect or missing letter would be.

 Essential

The only exception to the rules about accents was capital letters, which were often left unaccented. However, this usage has changed with computers replacing typewriters, and it's a good idea to always use them on capital letters in order to spell the word correctly and avoid confusion between words like *SALE* (dirty) and *SALÉ* (salted).

The *accent aigu* (acute accent) is found only on the letter *e*. At the beginning of a word, it often indicates that in Old French, an *s* used to follow that vowel, e.g., *écolee* (school).

The *accent grave* (grave accent) may be used on *a*, *e*, or *u*. On the *a* and *u*, it usually serves to distinguish between homonyms; e.g., *a* (third person singular of *avoir*) versus à (preposition "at").

The *accent circonflexe* (circumflex) can be on any vowel. The circumflex usually indicates that in Old French, an *s* used to follow that vowel, e.g., *hôpital* (hospital). The circumflex can also distinguish between homonyms; e.g., *du* (contraction of *de* + *le*) versus *dû* (past participle of *devoir*).

The *accent tréma* (dieresis or umlaut) can be on *e*, *i*, or *u*. It is used when two vowels are next to each other and both must be pronounced, e.g., naïve, Noël.

The *cédille* (cedilla) is found only on the letter *c*. It changes a hard *c* sound (like *k*) into a soft *c* sound (like *s*), e.g., *leçon* (lesson). We never put a cedilla in front of *e* or *i*, because *c* is always soft in front of these vowels.

Contractions

Contractions—the dropping of one or more letters and replacing them with an apostrophe—are optional in English but required in French. For example, in English you can say "I am" or "I'm"; the latter is somewhat less formal. In contrast, you cannot say "*je ai*" (I have) in French; you must make the contraction *j'ai*. There are three main types of French contractions:

1. Short, single-syllable words contract with the word that follows if it begins with a vowel or *h muet*.

ce + est	*c'est*	it is
de + amour	*d'amour*	of/about love
je + habite	*j'habite*	I live
je le + ai	*je l'ai*	I have it

la + amie	l'amie	the friend
le + homme	l'homme	the man
il me + adore	il m'adore	he adores me
il ne + est pas	il n'est pas	it isn't
que + il	qu'il	that it/ that he
il se + appelle	il s'appelle	his name is
je te + aime	je t'aime	I love you

2. The prepositions *à* and *de* contract with the definite articles *le* and *les*, but not with *la* or *l'*:

À

à + le	au
à + les	aux
à + la	à la
à + l'	à l'

DE

de + le	du
de + les	des
de + la	de la
de + l'	de l'

3. *Si* contracts with *il* and *ils*, but not *elle(s)*:

si + il	s'il	if he/it
si + ils	s'ils	if they
si + elle	si elle	if she/it
si + elles	si elles	if they

Capitalization

Capitalization is far less common in French than in English. Take note of the following groups of words which are capitalized in English but not in French:

- First person singular subject pronoun:
  Il a dit « j'ai faim ». He said, "I'm hungry."
- Days of the week:
  lundi, mardi . . . —Monday, Tuesday . . .
- Months of the year:
  janvier, février . . . —January, February . . .
- Geographical words:
  l'océan Atlantique—Atlantic Ocean,
  rue Molière—Molière Street
- Languages:
  le français, l'anglais—French, English
- Nationalities as adjectives:
  un drapeau canadien—Canadian flag
- Religion:
  le christianisme, un musulman—Christianity, a Muslim

Question?

What is capitalized in French?
The first word in a sentence, proper names (Mme Dubois), titles, and nationalities as nouns (*un Américain*) are all capitalized in French.

Punctuation

French and English use most of the same punctuation marks, but the way that they are used in the two languages can be quite different.

One-part Punctuation

One-part punctuation marks are very similar in the two languages, so the summary for punctuation usage only covers the differences between French punctuation usage and that of English.

Period

The period (*le point*, in French) is used in some French countries and parts of Canada to separate numbers, rather than the comma that is used in English: *10.500*—10,500. In France, however, a space is used in place of the English comma to separate thousands, for example, so a number such as 123,456 would become in French 123 456. The period can also be used in French to separate dates: *6.12.05*—6 décembre 2005. The period is not used after abbreviations of measurement, abbreviated titles, or as a decimal point: *20 min*–20 minutes, *Mme*—Mrs. (However for "Monsieur" the correct abbreviation is "M.")

Comma

The comma (*la virgule*, in French) is equivalent to the decimal point used in English: *7,25 %*—7.25%.

Two-part Punctuation Marks

In French, all punctuation marks and symbols with two or more parts, such as : ; « » ! ? % $ and #, must be preceded by a space: *Ça va ? Très bien !*

Colon

The colon, called *les deux points* in French, is much more common in French than in English. It is used to introduce direct speech, where in English you would use a comma: *Il a dit : « Je veux le faire ».*—He said, "I want to do it."

The colon can also introduce the explanation, conclusion, or summary of whatever precedes it: *Ce livre est très bon : c'est un classique du genre.* This book is very good; it's a classic of its kind.

Quotation marks

Quotation marks (*les guillemets*) tend to be used only at the beginning and end of an entire conversation. This is quite different than the use of quotation marks in English, which surrounds each spoken word, phrase, or paragraph with quotation marks, which means that the quotation marks end each time there is an incidental clause like "he said" or "she replied," as well as any time the speaker changes. This is not the case in French. Instead, *les guillemets* surround the entire conversation and each new speaker is indicated by an m-dash (*un tiret*).

> « *Salut Marc ! dit Anne. Ça va ?*
> —*Ah, salut Anne ! répond Marc. Ça va bien, et toi ?*
> —*Oui, ça va* ».

Similarities
The following symbols are used more or less the same way in French and English, besides the fact that French inserts a space between last letter and punctuation mark:

- *le point-virgule* (semi-colon)
- *le point d'exclamation* (exclamation point)
- *le point d'interrogation* (question mark)

Spelling Equivalents

There are certain spelling equivalents which can help you identify French and English cognates. That is, certain spelling patterns (usually suffixes) in one language equal spelling patterns in the other language. The following table lists common spelling equivalents between the two languages.

FRENCH	ENGLISH	FRENCH EXAMPLE	ENGLISH TRANSLATION
^	_s	*forêt, bête*	forest, beast
-*ain(e)*	-an	*Américain(e)*	American
-*ais(e)*	-ese	*Japonais(e)*	Japanese
-*ance*	-ence	*dépendance*	dependence

FRENCH	ENGLISH	FRENCH EXAMPLE	ENGLISH TRANSLATION
-ant	-ent	indépendant	independent
-çon	-sson	leçon	lesson
	-shion	façon	fashion
	-son	maçon	mason
é-	s-	état, école	state, school
-e	-y	victoire	victory
-é(e)	-ed	arrivé	arrived
-é	-y	qualité	quality
-el(le)	-al	personnel (le)	personal
		éternel(le)	eternal
-en(ne)	-an	Canadien(ne)	Canadian
-ant	-ing	en arrivant	arriving
		en finissant	finishing
-ence	-ence	violence	violence
-ent	-ent	apparent	apparent
-er	to + verb	arriver	to arrive
-eur	-or	acteur	actor
	-or/-our	couleur	color/colour
	-er	employeur	employer
-eux/euse	-ous	nerveux	nervous
-i	-y	parti	party
-i(e)	-ed, -t	fini(e)	finished
-if/ive	-ive	positif(ive), motif	positive, motive
-ique	-ic	musique	music
	-ical	lyrique	lyrical
-ir	to + verb	finir	to finish
-isation	-ization	réalisation	realization
	-isation		realisation
-iser	-ize	idéaliser	idealize
-iste	-ist	optimiste	optimist/optimistic
-ment	-ly	rapidement	rapidly
-oire	-ory	obligatoire	obligatory
		mémoire	memory
-ois(e)	-ese	Chinois(e)	Chinese

FRENCH	ENGLISH	FRENCH EXAMPLE	ENGLISH TRANSLATION
-re	-er	mètre	meter/metre
	-re	théâtre	theater/theatre
-re	to + verb	répondre	to respond
-tion	-tion	nation	nation
-u(e)	-ed	répondu	responded

Be aware that the common spelling elements for French and English are just guidelines to spelling equivalents between French and English, not hard and fast rules. There are many exceptions!

Acronyms and Abbreviations

Acronyms and abbreviations can be difficult, because not only do you have to know what the letters stand for, you also have to know what the spelled out words mean. Here are some common acronyms.

AR	accusé/avis de réception	return receipt requested
A.R.	aller-retour	round trip
BCBG	bon chic bon genre	preppy
BD	bande dessinée	comic strip
BP	boîte postale	post office box
CB	carte bleue	Visa card
CCP	compte chèque postal	postal checking account
Cie	compagnie	Co.
CP	cours préparatoire	kindergarten
CV	curriculum vitae	résumé
DALF	diplôme approfondi de langue française	Test of English as a Foreign Language (TOEFL)
DEA	diplôme d'études approfondies	Ph.D. minus the dissertation
DELF	diplôme d'études en langue française	TOEFL
DES	diplôme d'études supérieures	Master's degree
DEUG	diplôme d'études universitaires générales	Associate's degree
EDF	Électricité de France	nationalized French electric company
GAB	guichet automatique de banque	ATM, cash dispenser

GDF	Gaz de France	nationalized French gas company
Go	giga-octet	GB (gigabyte)
HLM	Habitation à loyer modéré	low-income housing
HS	Hors service	out of order
HT	Hors taxe	tax not included
IVG	interruption volontaire de grossesse	abortion
Mo	mega-octet	MB (megabyte)
ONG	organisation non gouvernementale	NGO
ONU	Organisation des Nations unies	UN
OVNI	Objet volant non identifié	UFO
PC	poste de commandement	HQ
Pcc	pour copie conforme	certified copy
PCV	paiement contre vérification or percevoir	collect call
PDG	président-directeur général	CEO
PEL	plan d'épargne logement	savings account
PIB	produit intérieur brut	GDP (gross domestic product)
PNB	produit national brut	GNP (gross national product)
qcm	questionnaire à choix multiple	multiple choice test
Q.G.	quartier général	HQ (military headquarters), local pub
RATP	Régie autonome des transports parisiens	Parisian public transit (métro and bus)
rdc	rez-de-chaussée	first floor (US), ground floor (UK)
RER	Réseau express régional	train service between Paris and suburbs
RMI	revenu minimum d'insertion	welfare
RN	route nationale	main road
RN	revenu national	GNP
RSVP	répondez s'il vous plaît	please respond

Alert!

The letters *RSVP* stand for *répondez s'il vous plaît*, which means that "please RSVP" is redundant in English.

rv	rendez-vous	meeting, date
SDF	Sans domicile fixe	homeless (noun or adjective)
Sida	syndrome immunodéficitaire acquis	AIDS
SMIC	salaire minimum interprofessionnel de croissance	minimum wage
SNCF	Société nationale des chemins de fer	nationalized French train system
SVP	s'il vous plaît	please
TGV	train à grande vitesse	high-speed train
TTC	toutes taxes comprises	tax included
TVA	taxe à la valeur ajoutée	VAT (value-added tax)
U.E.	Union européenne	EU (European Union)
U.V.	unité de valeur	university course credit
v.f.	version française	film dubbed into French
v.o.	version originale	film shown in its original language usually with subtitles in French
VTT	vélo tout terrain	mountain bike
W.-C.	water-closet	toilet

Apocopes

Apocopes, which are words that have one or more syllables cut off the end, are also common in French. The following apocopes are considered "normal register"—you can use them when talking to anyone. Note that many apocopes have to do with school, work, transportation, and technology.

l'art déco	les arts décoratifs	decorative arts
une auto	une automobile	car
bio	biologique	organic
la dactylo	la dactylographie	typing
la gym	la gymnastique	gym, P.E.
un kilo	un kilogramme	kilogram, 2.2 pounds
le magnéto	le magnétophone	tape recorder
la météo	la météorologie	weather forecast, report
le métro	le métropolitain	subway
un micro	un microphone	mike, microphone

une moto	une motocyclette	motorbike
une photo	une photographie	photograph
un pneu	un pneumatique	tire, tyre
la prog	la progression	progress, growth
un pull	un pull-over	sweater, jumper
une sténo	une sténographe	stenographer
une stéréo	une/ chaîne stéréophonique	stereo
un vélo	un vélocipède (archaic)	bike, bicycle

These next apocopes are informal, so you should only use them with people you are on familiar terms with.

un ado	un adolescent	teenager, adolescent
un apéro	un apéritif	cocktail, before dinner drink
un appart	un appartement	apartment, flat
cet(te) aprèm	cet(te) après-midi	this afternoon
un bac	un baccalauréat	high school diploma, A-levels
un beauf	un beau-frère	brother-in-law, small-minded person
le champ (pronounce the final "p")	le champagne	champagne, bubbly
un ciné	un cinéma	movie theater
d'acc ! dac !	D'accord !	OK!
déca, DK	décaféiné	decaf
un dico	un dictionnaire	dictionary
un exam	un examen	test, exam
extra	extraordinaire	terrific, great
la fac	la faculté	university department, university
le foot	le football	soccer, football
un frigo	un réfrigérateur	fridge, refrigerator
le gaspi	le gaspillage	waste
la géo	la géographie	geography
un hosto	un hôpital	hospital
impec	impeccable	terrific

un imper	un imperméable	raincoat, mac
une info	une information	piece of information
les maths	les mathématiques	math
un ordi	un ordinateur	computer
le petit déj'	le petit déjeuner	breakfast
la philo	la philosophie	philosophy
un prof	un professeur	teacher
un/e proprio	un/e propriétaire	landlord/lady
la pub	la publicité	ad, advertising
un resto	un restaurant	restaurant
les sciences po	les sciences politiques	political science
la Sécu	Sécurité sociale	Social Security, Medicaid
sensass	sensationnel	fantastic, terrific
sympa	sympathique	nice, friendly
la télé	la télévision	TV, telly
l'uni (more used in Québec and Switzerland)	l'université	university
un/e véto	un/e vétérinaire	vet, veterinarian

Verb Tables

ALLER

to go / Irregular verb

	Présent	Subjonctif
je/j'	vais	aille
tu	vas	ailles
il / elle	va	aille
nous	allons	allions
vous	allez	alliez
ils / elles	vont	aillent
	Imparfait	**Passé simple**
j'	allais	allai
tu	allais	allas
il / elle	allait	alla
nous	allions	allâmes
vous	alliez	allâtes
ils / elles	allaient	allèrent
	Futur	**Conditionnel**
j'	irai	irais
tu	iras	irais
il / elle	ira	irait
nous	irons	irions
vous	irez	iriez
ils / elles	iront	iraient
	Imparfait du subjonctif	**Impératif**
j'	allasse	
tu	allasses	va
il / elle	allât	
nous	allassions	allons
vous	allassiez	allez
ils / elles	allassent	
Auxiliaire	**Participe passé**	**Participe présent**
être	allé	allant

APPELER

to call / Stem-changing (L > LL) -ER verb
s'appeler—to be called/named

	Présent	Subjonctif
j'	appelle	appelle
tu	appelles	appelles
il / elle	appelle	appelle
nous	appelons	appelions
vous	appelez	appeliez
ils / elles	appellent	appellent
	Imparfait	**Passé simple**
j'	appelais	appelai
tu	appelais	appelas
il / elle	appelait	appela
nous	appelions	appelâmes
vous	appeliez	appelâtes
ils / elles	appelaient	appelèrent
	Futur	**Conditionnel**
j'	appellerai	appellerais
tu	appelleras	appellerais
il / elle	appellera	appellerait
nous	appellerons	appellerions
vous	appellerez	appelleriez
ils / elles	appelleront	appelleraient
	Imparfait du subjonctif	**Impératif**
j'	appelasse	
tu	appelasses	appelle
il / elle	appelât	
nous	appelassions	appelons
vous	appelassiez	appelez
ils/elle	appelassent	
Auxiliaire	**Participe passé**	**Participe présent**
avoir	appelé	appelant

AVOIR

to have / Irregular verb

	Présent	Subjonctif
j'	ai	aie
tu	as	aies
il / elle	a	ait
nous	avons	ayons
vous	avez	ayez
ils / elles	ont	aient
	Imparfait	**Passé simple**
j'	avais	eus
tu	avais	eus
il / elle	avait	eut
nous	avions	eûmes
vous	aviez	eûtes
ils / elles	avaient	eurent
	Futur	**Conditionnel**
j'	aurai	aurais
tu	auras	aurais
il / elle	aura	aurait
nous	aurons	aurions
vous	aurez	auriez
ils / elles	auront	auraient
	Imparfait du subjonctif	**Impératif**
j'	eusse	
tu	eusses	aie
il / elle	eût	
nous	eussions	ayons
vous	eussiez	ayez
ils / elles	eussent	
Auxiliaire	**Participe passé**	**Participe présent**
avoir	eu	ayant

Things To Do

- [ ]
- [ ]
- [ ]
- [ ]
- [ ]
- [ ]
- [ ]
- [ ]
- [ ]
- [ ]
- [ ]

BATTRE

to beat / Regular -RE verb except in *présent* and *impératif*

	Présent	Subjonctif
je	bats	batte
tu	bats	battes
il / elle	bat	batte
nous	battons	battions
vous	battez	battiez
ils / elles	battent	battent
	Imparfait	**Passé simple**
je	battais	battis
tu	battais	battis
il / elle	battait	battit
nous	battions	battîmes
vous	battiez	battîtes
ils / elles	battaient	battirent
	Futur	**Conditionnel**
je	battrai	battrais
tu	battras	battrais
il / elle	battra	battrait
nous	battrons	battrions
vous	battrez	battriez
ils / elles	battront	battraient
	Imparfait du subjonctif	**Impératif**
je	battisse	
tu	battisses	bats
il / elle	battît	
nous	battissions	battons
vous	battissiez	battez
ils / elles	battissent	
Auxiliaire	**Participe passé**	**Participe présent**
avoir	battu	battant

THE EVERYTHING FRENCH GRAMMAR BOOK

CHOISIR

to choose / Regular -IR verb

	Présent	Subjonctif
je	choisis	choisisse
tu	choisis	choisisses
il / elle	choisit	choisisse
nous	choisissons	choisissions
vous	choisissez	choisissiez
ils / elles	choisissent	choisissent
	Imparfait	**Passé simple**
je	choisissais	choisis
tu	choisissais	choisis
il / elle	choisissait	choisit
nous	choisissions	choisîmes
vous	choisissiez	choisîtes
ils / elles	choisissaient	choisirent
	Futur	**Conditionnel**
je	choisirai	choisirais
tu	choisiras	choisirais
il / elle	choisira	choisirait
nous	choisirons	choisirions
vous	choisirez	choisiriez
ils / elles	choisiront	choisiraient
	Imparfait du subjonctif	**Impératif**
je	choisisse	
tu	choisisses	choisis
il / elle	choisît	
nous	choisissions	choisissons
vous	choisissiez	choisissez
ils / elles	choisissent	
Auxiliaire	**Participe passé**	**Participe présent**
avoir	choisi	choisissant

CONNAÎTRE

to know, be familiar with / Irregular -RE verb

	Présent	Subjonctif
je	connais	connaisse
tu	connais	connaisses
il / elle	connaît	connaisse
nous	connaissons	connaissions
vous	connaissez	connaissiez
ils / elles	connaissent	connaissent
	Imparfait	**Passé simple**
je	connaissais	connus
tu	connaissais	connus
il / elle	connaissait	connut
nous	connaissions	connûmes
vous	connaissiez	connûtes
ils / elles	connaissaient	connurent
	Futur	**Conditionnel**
je	connaîtrai	connaîtrais
tu	connaîtras	connaîtrais
il / elle	connaîtra	connaîtrait
nous	connaîtrons	connaîtrions
vous	connaîtrez	connaîtriez
ils / elles	connaîtront	connaîtraient
	Imparfait du subjonctif	**Impératif**
je	connusse	
tu	connusses	connais
il / elle	connût	
nous	connussions	connaissons
vous	connussiez	connaissez
ils / elles	connussent	
Auxiliaire	**Participe passé**	**Participe présent**
avoir	connu	connaissant

CONSIDÉRER

to consider / Stem-changing (É > È) -ER verb

	Présent	Subjonctif
je	considère	considère
tu	considères	considères
il / elle	considère	considère
nous	considérons	considérions
vous	considérez	considériez
ils / elles	considèrent	considèrent
	Imparfait	**Passé simple**
je	considérais	considérai
tu	considérais	considéras
il / elle	considérait	considéra
nous	considérions	considérâmes
vous	considériez	considérâtes
ils / elles	considéraient	considérèrent
	Futur	**Conditionnel**
je	considérerai	considérerais
tu	considéreras	considérerais
il / elle	considérera	considérerait
nous	considérerons	considérerions
vous	considérerez	considéreriez
ils / elles	considéreront	considéreraient
	Imparfait du subjonctif	**Impératif**
je	considérasse	
tu	considérasses	considère
il / elle	considérât	
nous	considérassions	considérons
vous	considérassiez	considérez
ils / elles	considérassent	
Auxiliaire	**Participe passé**	**Participe présent**
avoir	considéré	considérant

DESCENDRE

to go down, descend / Regular -RE verb

	Présent	Subjonctif
je	descends	descende
tu	descends	descendes
il / elle	descend	descende
nous	descendons	descendions
vous	descendez	descendiez
ils / elles	descendent	descendent
	Imparfait	**Passé simple**
je	descendais	descendis
tu	descendais	descendis
il / elle	descendait	descendit
nous	descendions	descendîmes
vous	descendiez	descendîtes
ils / elles	descendaient	descendirent
	Futur	**Conditionnel**
je	descendrai	descendrais
tu	descendras	descendrais
il / elle	descendra	descendrait
nous	descendrons	descendrions
vous	descendrez	descendriez
ils / elles	descendront	descendraient
	Imparfait du subjonctif	**Impératif**
je	descendisse	
tu	descendisses	descends
il / elle	descendît	
nous	descendissions	descendons
vous	descendissiez	descendez
ils / elles	descendissent	
Auxiliaire	**Participe passé**	**Participe présent**
être	descendu	descendant

DEVOIR

should, must, to have to / Irregular -IR verb

	Présent	Subjonctif
je	dois	doive
tu	dois	doives
il / elle	doit	doive
nous	devons	devions
vous	devez	deviez
ils / elles	doivent	doivent
	Imparfait	**Passé simple**
je	devais	dus
tu	devais	dus
il / elle	devait	dut
nous	devions	dûmes
vous	deviez	dûtes
ils / elles	devaient	durent
	Futur	**Conditionnel**
je	devrai	devrais
tu	devras	devrais
il / elle	devra	devrait
nous	devrons	devrions
vous	devrez	devriez
ils / elles	devront	devraient
	Imparfait du subjonctif	**Impératif**
je	dusse	
tu	dusses	dois
il / elle	dût	
nous	dussions	devons
vous	dussiez	devez
ils / elles	dussent	
Auxiliaire	**Participe passé**	**Participe présent**
avoir	dû	devant

DORMIR

to sleep / Irregular -IR verb

	Présent	Subjonctif
je	dors	dorme
tu	dors	dormes
il / elle	dort	dorme
nous	dormons	dormions
vous	dormez	dormiez
ils / elles	dorment	dorment
	Imparfait	**Passé simple**
je	dormais	dormis
tu	dormais	dormis
il / elle	dormait	dormit
nous	dormions	dormîmes
vous	dormiez	dormîtes
ils / elles	dormaient	dormirent
	Futur	**Conditionnel**
je	dormirai	dormirais
tu	dormiras	dormirais
il / elle	dormira	dormirait
nous	dormirons	dormirions
vous	dormirez	dormiriez
ils / elles	dormiront	dormiraient
	Imparfait du subjonctif	**Impératif**
je	dormisse	
tu	dormisses	dors
il / elle	dormît	
nous	dormissions	dormons
vous	dormissiez	dormez
ils / elles	dormissent	
Auxiliaire	**Participe passé**	**Participe présent**
avoir	dormi	dormant

ÊTRE

to be / Irregular -RE verb

	Présent	Subjonctif
je	suis	sois
tu	es	sois
il / elle	est	soit
nous	sommes	soyons
vous	êtes	soyez
ils / elles	sont	soient
	Imparfait	**Passé simple**
j'/je	étais	fus
tu	étais	fus
il / elle	était	fut
nous	étions	fûmes
vous	étiez	fûtes
ils / elles	étaient	furent
	Futur	**Conditionnel**
je	serai	serais
tu	seras	serais
il / elle	sera	serait
nous	serons	serions
vous	serez	seriez
ils / elles	seront	seraient
	Imparfait du subjonctif	**Impératif**
je	fusse	
tu	fusses	sois
il / elle	fût	
nous	fussions	soyons
vous	fussiez	soyez
ils / elles	fussent	
Auxiliaire	**Participe passé**	**Participe présent**
avoir	été	étant

ÉTUDIER

to study / Regular -ER verb

	Présent	**Subjonctif**
j'	*étudie*	*étudie*
tu	*étudies*	*étudies*
il / elle	*étudie*	*étudie*
nous	*étudions*	*étudiions*
vous	*étudiez*	*étudiiez*
ils / elles	*étudient*	*étudient*
	Imparfait	**Passé simple**
j'	*étudiais*	*étudiai*
tu	*étudiais*	*étudias*
il / elle	*étudiait*	*étudia*
nous	*étudiions*	*étudiâmes*
vous	*étudiiez*	*étudiâtes*
ils / elles	*étudiaient*	*étudièrent*
	Futur	**Conditionnel**
j'	*étudierai*	*étudierais*
tu	*étudieras*	*étudierais*
il / elle	*étudiera*	*étudierait*
nous	*étudierons*	*étudierions*
vous	*étudierez*	*étudieriez*
ils / elles	*étudieront*	*étudieraient*
	Imparfait du subjonctif	**Impératif**
j'	*étudiasse*	
tu	*étudiasses*	*étudie*
il / elle	*étudiât*	
nous	*étudiassions*	*étudions*
vous	*étudiassiez*	*étudiez*
ils / elles	*étudiassent*	
Auxiliaire	**Participe passé**	**Participe présent**
avoir	*étudié*	*étudiant*

FAIRE

to make, to do / Irregular -RE verb

	Présent	Subjonctif
je	fais	fasse
tu	fais	fasses
il / elle	fait	fasse
nous	faisons	fassions
vous	faites	fassiez
ils / elles	font	fassent
	Imparfait	**Passé simple**
je	faisais	fis
tu	faisais	fis
il / elle	faisait	fit
nous	faisions	fîmes
vous	faisiez	fîtes
ils / elles	faisaient	firent
	Futur	**Conditionnel**
je	ferai	ferais
tu	feras	ferais
il / elle	fera	ferait
nous	ferons	ferions
vous	ferez	feriez
ils / elles	feront	feraient
	Imparfait du subjonctif	**Impératif**
je	fisse	
tu	fisses	fais
il / elle	fît	
nous	fissions	faisons
vous	fissiez	faites
ils / elles	fissent	
Auxiliaire	**Participe passé**	**Participe présent**
avoir	fait	faisant

JETER

to throw / Stem-changing (T > TT) -ER verb

	Présent	Subjonctif
je	jette	jette
tu	jettes	jettes
il / elle	jette	jette
nous	jetons	jetions
vous	jetez	jetiez
ils / elles	jettent	jettent
	Imparfait	**Passé simple**
je	jetais	jetai
tu	jetais	jetas
il / elle	jetait	jeta
nous	jetions	jetâmes
vous	jetiez	jetâtes
ils / elles	jetaient	jetèrent
	Futur	**Conditionnel**
je	jetterai	jetterais
tu	jetteras	jetterais
il / elle	jettera	jetterait
nous	jetterons	jetterions
vous	jetterez	jetteriez
ils / elles	jetteront	jetteraient
	Imparfait du subjonctif	**Impératif**
je	jetasse	
tu	jetasses	jette
il / elle	jetât	
nous	jetassions	jetons
vous	jetassiez	jetez
ils / elles	jetassent	
Auxiliaire	**Participe passé**	**Participe présent**
avoir	jeté	jetant

LANCER

to throw / Spelling-change (C > Ç) -ER verb

	Présent	Subjonctif
je	lance	lance
tu	lances	lances
il / elle	lance	lance
nous	lançons	lancions
vous	lancez	lanciez
ils / elles	lancent	lancent
	Imparfait	**Passé simple**
je	lançais	lançai
tu	lançais	lanças
il / elle	lançait	lança
nous	lancions	lançâmes
vous	lanciez	lançâtes
ils / elles	lançaient	lancèrent
	Futur	**Conditionnel**
je	lancerai	lancerais
tu	lanceras	lancerais
il / elle	lancera	lancerait
nous	lancerons	lancerions
vous	lancerez	lanceriez
ils / elles	lanceront	lanceraient
	Imparfait du subjonctif	**Impératif**
je	lançasse	
tu	lançasses	lance
il / elle	lançât	
nous	lançassions	lançons
vous	lançassiez	lancez
ils / elles	lançassent	
Auxiliaire	**Participe passé**	**Participe présent**
avoir	lancé	lançant

LEVER

to lift, raise / Stem-changing (E > È) -ER verb
se lever—to get up

	Présent	Subjonctif
je	lève	lève
tu	lèves	lèves
il / elle	lève	lève
nous	levons	levions
vous	levez	leviez
ils / elles	lèvent	lèvent
	Imparfait	**Passé simple**
je	levais	levai
tu	levais	levas
il / elle	levait	leva
nous	levions	levâmes
vous	leviez	levâtes
ils / elles	levaient	levèrent
	Futur	**Conditionnel**
je	lèverai	lèverais
tu	lèveras	lèverais
il / elle	lèvera	lèverait
nous	lèverons	lèverions
vous	lèverez	lèveriez
ils / elles	lèveront	lèveraient
	Imparfait du subjonctif	**Impératif**
je	levasse	
tu	levasses	lève
il / elle	levât	
nous	levassions	levons
vous	levassiez	levez
ils / elles	levassent	
Auxiliaire	**Participe passé**	**Participe présent**
avoir	levé	levant

MANGER

to eat / Spelling-change (G > GE) -ER verb

	Présent	Subjonctif
je	mange	mange
tu	manges	manges
il / elle	mange	mange
nous	mangeons	mangions
vous	mangez	mangiez
ils / elles	mangent	mangent
	Imparfait	**Passé simple**
je	mangeais	mangeai
tu	mangeais	mangeas
il / elle	mangeait	mangea
nous	mangions	mangeâmes
vous	mangiez	mangeâtes
ils / elles	mangeaient	mangèrent
	Futur	**Conditionnel**
je	mangerai	mangerais
tu	mangeras	mangerais
il / elle	mangera	mangerait
nous	mangerons	mangerions
vous	mangerez	mangeriez
ils / elles	mangeront	mangeraient
	Imparfait du subjonctif	**Impératif**
je	mangeasse	
tu	mangeasses	mange
il / elle	mangeât	
nous	mangeassions	mangeons
vous	mangeassiez	mangez
ils / elles	mangeassent	
Auxiliaire	**Participe passé**	**Participe présent**
avoir	mangé	mangeant

SE MOQUER

to mock, make fun of / Reflexive regular -ER verb

	Présent	Subjonctif
je me	moque	moque
tu te	moques	moques
il / elle se	moque	moque
nous nous	moquons	moquions
vous vous	moquez	moquiez
ils / elles se	moquent	moquent
	Imparfait	**Passé simple**
je me	moquais	moquai
tu te	moquais	moquas
il / elle se	moquait	moqua
nous nous	moquions	moquâmes
vous vous	moquiez	moquâtes
ils / elles se	moquaient	moquèrent
	Futur	**Conditionnel**
je me	moquerai	moquerais
tu te	moqueras	moquerais
il / elle se	moquera	moquerait
nous nous	moquerons	moquerions
vous vous	moquerez	moqueriez
ils / elles se	moqueront	moqueraient
	Imparfait du subjonctif	**Impératif**
je me	moquasse	
tu te	moquasses	moque-toi
il / elle se	moquât	
nous nous	moquassions	moquons-nous
vous vous	moquassiez	moquez-vous
ils / elles se	moquassent	
Auxiliaire	**Participe passé**	**Participe présent**
s'être	moqué	se moquant

NETTOYER

to clean / Stem-changing (Y > I) -ER verb

	Présent	Subjonctif
je	nettoie	nettoie
tu	nettoies	nettoies
il / elle	nettoie	nettoie
nous	nettoyons	nettoyions
vous	nettoyez	nettoyiez
ils / elles	nettoient	nettoient
	Imparfait	**Passé simple**
je	nettoyais	nettoyai
tu	nettoyais	nettoyas
il / elle	nettoyait	nettoya
nous	nettoyions	nettoyâmes
vous	nettoyiez	nettoyâtes
ils / elles	nettoyaient	nettoyèrent
	Futur	**Conditionnel**
je	nettoierai	nettoierais
tu	nettoieras	nettoierais
il / elle	nettoiera	nettoierait
nous	nettoierons	nettoierions
vous	nettoierez	nettoieriez
ils / elles	nettoieront	nettoieraient
	Imparfait du subjonctif	**Impératif**
je	nettoyasse	
tu	nettoyasses	nettoie
il / elle	nettoyât	
nous	nettoyassions	nettoyons
vous	nettoyassiez	nettoyez
ils / elles	nettoyassent	
Auxiliaire	**Participe passé**	**Participe présent**
avoir	nettoyé	nettoyant

OUVRIR

to open / Irregular -IR verb

	Présent	Subjonctif
j'	ouvre	ouvre
tu	ouvres	ouvres
il / elle	ouvre	ouvre
nous	ouvrons	ouvrions
vous	ouvrez	ouvriez
ils / elles	ouvrent	ouvrent
	Imparfait	**Passé simple**
j'	ouvrais	ouvris
tu	ouvrais	ouvris
il / elle	ouvrait	ouvrit
nous	ouvrions	ouvrîmes
vous	ouvriez	ouvrîtes
ils / elles	ouvraient	ouvrirent
	Futur	**Conditionnel**
j'	ouvrirai	ouvrirais
tu	ouvriras	ouvrirais
il / elle	ouvrira	ouvrirait
nous	ouvrirons	ouvririons
vous	ouvrirez	ouvririez
ils / elles	ouvriront	ouvriraient
	Imparfait du subjonctif	**Impératif**
j'	ouvrisse	
tu	ouvrisses	ouvre
il / elle	ouvrît	
nous	ouvrissions	ouvrons
vous	ouvrissiez	ouvrez
ils / elles	ouvrissent	
Auxiliaire	**Participe passé**	**Participe présent**
avoir	ouvert	ouvrant

PARLER

to talk, speak / Regular -ER verb

	Présent	Subjonctif
je	parle	parle
tu	parles	parles
il / elle	parle	parle
nous	parlons	parlions
vous	parlez	parliez
ils / elles	parlent	parlent
	Imparfait	**Passé simple**
je	parlais	parlai
tu	parlais	parlas
il / elle	parlait	parla
nous	parlions	parlâmes
vous	parliez	parlâtes
ils / elles	parlaient	parlèrent
	Futur	**Conditionnel**
je	parlerai	parlerais
tu	parleras	parlerais
il / elle	parlera	parlerait
nous	parlerons	parlerions
vous	parlerez	parleriez
ils / elles	parleront	parleraient
	Imparfait du subjonctif	**Impératif**
je	parlasse	
tu	parlasses	parle
il / elle	parlât	
nous	parlassions	parlons
vous	parlassiez	parlez
ils / elles	parlassent	
Auxiliaire	**Participe passé**	**Participe présent**
avoir	parlé	parlant

PAYER

to pay / Optional stem-changing (Y > I) -ER verb

	Présent	Subjonctif
je	paie / paye	paie / paye
tu	paies / payes	paies / payes
il / elle	paie / paye	paie / paye
nous	payons	payions
vous	payez	payiez
ils / elles	paient / payent	paient / payent
	Imparfait	**Passé simple**
je	payais	payai
tu	payais	payas
il / elle	payait	paya
nous	payions	payâmes
vous	payiez	payâtes
ils / elles	payaient	payèrent
	Futur	**Conditionnel**
je	paierai / payerai	paierais / payerais
tu	paieras / payeras	paierais / payerais
il / elle	paiera / payera	paierait / payerait
nous	paierons / payerons	paierions / payerions
vous	paierez / payerez	paieriez / payeriez
ils / elles	paieront / payeront	paieraient / payeraient
	Imparfait du subjonctif	**Impératif**
je	payasse	
tu	payasses	paie / paye
il / elle	payât	
nous	payassions	payons
vous	payassiez	payez
ils / elles	payassent	
Auxiliaire	**Participe passé**	**Participe présent**
avoir	payé	payant

POUVOIR

can, may, to be able to / Irregular verb

	Présent	Subjonctif
je	peux / puis	puisse
tu	peux	puisses
il / elle	peut	puisse
nous	pouvons	puissions
vous	pouvez	puissiez
ils / elles	peuvent	puissent
	Imparfait	**Passé simple**
je	pouvais	pus
tu	pouvais	pus
il / elle	pouvait	put
nous	pouvions	pûmes
vous	pouviez	pûtes
ils / elles	pouvaient	purent
	Futur	**Conditionnel**
je	pourrai	pourrais
tu	pourras	pourrais
il / elle	pourra	pourrait
nous	pourrons	pourrions
vous	pourrez	pourriez
ils / elles	pourront	pourraient
	Imparfait du subjonctif	**Impératif**
je	pusse	
tu	pusses	n/a
il / elle	pût	
nous	pussions	
vous	pussiez	
ils / elles	pussent	
Auxiliaire	**Participe passé**	**Participe présent**
avoir	pu	pouvant

PRÉFÉRER

to prefer / Stem-changing (É > È) -ER verb

	Présent	Subjonctif
je	préfère	préfère
tu	préfères	préfères
il / elle	préfère	préfère
nous	préférons	préférions
vous	préférez	préfériez
ils / elles	préfèrent	préfèrent
	Imparfait	**Passé simple**
je	préférais	préférai
tu	préférais	préféras
il / elle	préférait	préféra
nous	préférions	préférâmes
vous	préfériez	préférâtes
ils / elles	préféraient	préférèrent
	Futur	**Conditionnel**
je	préférerai	préférerais
tu	préféreras	préférerais
il / elle	préférera	préférerait
nous	préférerons	préférerions
vous	préférerez	préféreriez
ils / elles	préféreront	préféreraient
	Imparfait du subjonctif	**Impératif**
je	préférasse	
tu	préférasses	préfère
il / elle	préférât	
nous	préférassions	préférons
vous	préférassiez	préférez
ils / elles	préférassent	
Auxiliaire	**Participe passé**	**Participe présent**
avoir	préféré	préférant

PRENDRE

to take / Irregular -RE verb

	Présent	Subjonctif
je	prends	prenne
tu	prends	prennes
il / elle	prend	prenne
nous	prenons	prenions
vous	prenez	preniez
ils / elles	prennent	prennent
	Imparfait	**Passé simple**
je	prenais	pris
tu	prenais	pris
il / elle	prenait	prit
nous	prenions	prîmes
vous	preniez	prîtes
ils / elles	prenaient	prirent
	Futur	**Conditionnel**
je	prendrai	prendrais
tu	prendras	prendrais
il / elle	prendra	prendrait
nous	prendrons	prendrions
vous	prendrez	prendriez
ils / elles	prendront	prendraient
	Imparfait du subjonctif	**Impératif**
je	prisse	
tu	prisses	prends
il / elle	prît	
nous	prissions	prenons
vous	prissiez	prenez
ils / elles	prissent	
Auxiliaire	**Participe passé**	**Participe présent**
avoir	pris	prenant

ROMPRE

to break / Regular -RE verb

	Présent	Subjonctif
je	romps	rompe
tu	romps	rompes
il / elle	romp	rompe
nous	rompons	rompions
vous	rompez	rompiez
ils / elles	rompent	rompent
	Imparfait	**Passé simple**
je	rompais	rompis
tu	rompais	rompis
il / elle	rompait	rompit
nous	rompions	rompîmes
vous	rompiez	rompîtes
ils / elles	rompaient	rompirent
	Futur	**Conditionnel**
je	romprai	romprais
tu	rompras	romprais
il / elle	rompra	romprait
nous	romprons	romprions
vous	romprez	rompriez
ils / elles	rompront	rompraient
	Imparfait du subjonctif	**Impératif**
je	rompisse	
tu	rompisses	romps
il / elle	rompît	
nous	rompissions	rompons
vous	rompissiez	rompez
ils / elles	rompissent	
Auxiliaire	**Participe passé**	**Participe présent**
avoir	rompu	rompant

SAVOIR

to know / Irregular -IR verb

	Présent	Subjonctif
je	sais	sache
tu	sais	saches
il / elle	sait	sache
nous	savons	sachions
vous	savez	sachiez
ils / elles	savent	sachent
	Imparfait	**Passé simple**
je	savais	sus
tu	savais	sus
il / elle	savait	sut
nous	savions	sûmes
vous	saviez	sûtes
ils / elles	savaient	surent
	Futur	**Conditionnel**
je	saurai	saurais
tu	sauras	saurais
il / elle	saura	saurait
nous	saurons	saurions
vous	saurez	sauriez
ils / elles	sauront	sauraient
	Imparfait su subjonctif	**Impératif**
je	susse	
tu	susses	sache
il / elle	sût	
nous	sussions	sachons
vous	sussiez	sachez
ils / elles	sussent	
Auxiliaire	**Participe passé**	**Participe présent**
avoir	su	sachant

VENDRE

to sell / Regular -RE verb

	Présent	Subjonctif
je	vends	vende
tu	vends	vendes
il / elle	vend	vende
nous	vendons	vendions
vous	vendez	vendiez
ils / elles	vendent	vendent
	Imparfait	**Passé simple**
je	vendais	vendis
tu	vendais	vendis
il / elle	vendait	vendit
nous	vendions	vendîmes
vous	vendiez	vendîtes
ils / elles	vendaient	vendirent
	Futur	**Conditionnel**
je	vendrai	vendrais
tu	vendras	vendrais
il / elle	vendra	vendrait
nous	vendrons	vendrions
vous	vendrez	vendriez
ils / elles	vendront	vendraient
	Imparfait du subjonctif	**Impératif**
je	vendisse	
tu	vendisses	vends
il / elle	vendît	
nous	vendissions	vendons
vous	vendissiez	vendez
ils / elles	vendissent	
Auxiliaire	**Participe passé**	**Participe présent**
avoir	vendu	vendant

VENIR

to come / Irregular -IR verb

	Présent	Subjonctif
je	viens	vienne
tu	viens	viennes
il / elle	vient	vienne
nous	venons	venions
vous	venez	veniez
ils / elles	viennent	viennent
	Imparfait	**Passé simple**
je	venais	vins
tu	venais	vins
il / elle	venait	vint
nous	venions	vînmes
vous	veniez	vîntes
ils / elles	venaient	vinrent
	Futur	**Conditionnel**
je	viendrai	viendrais
tu	viendras	viendrais
il / elle	viendra	viendrait
nous	viendrons	viendrions
vous	viendrez	viendriez
ils / elles	viendront	viendraient
	Imparfait du subjonctif	**Impératif**
je	vinsse	
tu	vinsses	viens
il / elle	vînt	
nous	vinssions	venons
vous	vinssiez	venez
ils / elles	vinssent	
Auxiliaire	**Participe passé**	**Participe présent**
être	venu	venant

VOULOIR

to want / Irregular verb

	Présent	Subjonctif
je	veux	veuille
tu	veux	veuilles
il / elle	veut	veuille
nous	voulons	voulions
vous	voulez	vouliez
ils / elles	veulent	veuillent
	Imparfait	**Passé simple**
je	voulais	voulus
tu	voulais	voulus
il / elle	voulait	voulut
nous	voulions	voulûmes
vous	vouliez	voulûtes
ils / elles	voulaient	voulurent
	Futur	**Conditionnel**
je	voudrai	voudrais
tu	voudras	voudrais
il / elle	voudra	voudrait
nous	voudrons	voudrions
vous	voudrez	voudriez
ils / elles	voudront	voudraient
	Imparfait du subjonctif	**Impératif**
je	voulusse	
tu	voulusses	veuille
il / elle	voulût	
nous	voulussions	n/a
vous	voulussiez	veuillez
ils / elles	voulussent	
Auxiliaire	**Participe passé**	**Participe présent**
avoir	voulu	voulant

Answer Key

CHAPTER 2

A.

1. *une étudiante*
2. *l'employée*
3. *une dentiste*
4. *les fonctionnaires*
5. *la cousine*
6. *des amies*
7. *les artistes*
8. *une patronne*
9. *l'Américaine*
10. *les traductrices*

B.

a. *des hommes*
b. *des femmes*
c. *les amis*
d. *les tartes*
e. *des salades*
f. *les idées*
g. *des manteaux*
h. *les feux*
i. *des gâteaux*
j. *les vies*

CHAPTER 3

A.

1. *noire, noirs, noires*
2. *grande, grands, grandes*
3. *petite, petits, petites*
4. *facile, faciles, faciles*
5. *grosse, gros, grosses*
6. *discrète, discrets, discrètes*
7. *franche, francs, franches*
8. *jalouse, jaloux, jalouses*
9. *bonne, bons, bonnes*
10. *tranquille, tranquilles, tranquilles*

B.

a. *la jolie fille*
b. *une robe verte*
c. *le garçon heureux*
d. *les jeunes cousines*
e. *des endroits idéaux (or idéals)*
f. *les bonnes amies*
g. *ces livres*
h. *quelle discussion intéressante*
i. *certaines nouvelles étudiantes*
j. *ces petites tables rouges*

CHAPTER 4

A.

1. *je, moi*
2. *tu, toi*
3. *il, lui*
4. *elle, elle*
5. *on, soi*
6. *nous, nous*

7. *vous, vous*
8. *ils, eux*
9. *elles, elles*
10. *il / elle, lui / elle*

B.

a. *celui-ci* (or just *celui*)—demonstrative
b. *celles-ci* (or *celles*)—demonstrative
c. *celui-là* (or *celui*)—demonstrative
d. *ceci*—indefinite demonstrative
e. *cela* (or *ça*)—indefinite demonstrative
f. *un autre*—indefinite
g. *chacun*—indefinite
h. *plusieurs*—indefinite
i. *quelque chose*—indefinite
j. *tout le monde*—indefinite

CHAPTER 5

A.

1. Conjugation refers to the different forms of verbs based on the five conjugation elements. The infinitive ending is the two-letter ending on French verbs that lets you know how to conjugate it. The radical is the infinitive minus the infinitive ending and is used as the basis of conjugation.
2. Number, person, tense, mood, voice
3. -er, -ir, -re
4. Present, past, future
5. Simple tenses are composed of a single word, while compound tenses have two or more words.
6. Indicative, subjunctive, imperative, conditional, infinitive, participle
7. Personal moods are conjugated according to the grammatical person performing the action, whereas impersonal moods are conjugated at the 3rd person singular
8. Active, passive, reflexive

9. -er verbs
10. Pronominal verbs must be preceded by a reflexive pronoun which indicates that the subject is performing the action of the verb upon itself. They can be recognized by the *se* which precedes the infinitive.

B.

a. infinitive
b. past participle of *rendre*
c. present participle of *abolir*
d. infinitive
e. infinitive
f. present participle of *chanter*
g. past participle of *choisir*
h. past participle of *entendre*
i. present participle of *penser*
j. infinitive

CHAPTER 6

1. *je chante, tu chantes, il chante, nous chantons, vous chantez, ils chantent*
2. *j'aime, tu aimes, il aime, nous aimons, vous aimez, ils aiment*
3. *je choisis, tu choisis, il choisit, nous choisissons, vous choisissez, ils choisissent*
4. *je finis, tu finis, il finit, nous finissons, vous finissez, ils finissent*
5. *je vends, tu vends, il vend, nous vendons, vous vendez, ils vendent*
6. *j'essaie, tu essaies, il essaie, nous essayons, vous essayez, ils essaient*
7. *je commence, tu commences, il commence, nous commençons, vous commencez, ils commencent*
8. *je me casse, tu te casses, il se casse, nous nous cassons, vous vous cassez, ils se cassent*
9. *je mets, tu mets, il met, nous mettons, vous mettez, ils mettent*

10. *je comprends, tu comprends, il comprend, nous comprenons, vous comprenez, ils comprennent*

CHAPTER 7

A.

1. to come
2. to have to
3. to know, be familiar with
4. to go
5. to be
6. to do, to make
7. to have
8. to know
9. to be able to, to be capable of
10. to want

B.

a. *Je dois savoir.*
b. *Il veut venir.*
c. *Nous allons manger.*
d. *Ils connaissent Cannes.*
e. *Vous pouvez étudier.*
f. *Elle a un frère.*
g. *Es - tu fatigué(e) ?*
h. *Il a raison.*
i. *Quel temps fait-il ?*
j. *Vous devez vraiment venir.*

CHAPTER 8

A.

1. *tu hantais*
2. *nous choisirons*
3. *elle vendrait*

4. *j'étais*
5. *vous danserez*
6. *ils finiraient*
7. *tu devras*
8. *il irait*
9. *nous serons*
10. *elles verraient*

B.

a. *attendant, attendu*
b. *étudiant, étudié*
c. *choisissant, choisi*
d. *allant, allé*
e. *étant, été*
f. *ayant, eu*
g. *comprenant, compris*
h. *sachant, su*
i. *pouvant, pu*
j. *coupant,, coupé*

CHAPTER 9

1. *j'ai aimé, tu as aimé, il a aimé, nous avons aimé, vous avez aimé, ils ont aimé*
2. *j'avais choisi, tu avais choisi, il avait choisi, nous avions choisi, vous aviez choisi, ils avaient choisi*
3. *j'aurai rendu, tu auras rendu, il aura rendu, nous aurons rendu, vous aurez rendu, ils auront rendu*
4. *j'avais appris, tu avais appris, il avait appris, nous avions appris, vous aviez appris, ils avaient appris*
5. *j'aurai pu, tu auras pu, il aura pu, nous aurons pu, vous aurez pu, ils auront pu*
6. *j'aurais su, tu aurais su, il aurait su, nous aurions su, vous auriez su, ils auraient su*
7. *j'étais sorti, tu étais sorti, il était sort, nous étions sortis, vous étiez sorti(s), ils étaient sortis*

8. *je suis monté, tu es monté, il est monté, nous sommes montés, vous êtes monté(s), ils sont montés*

9. *je serais venu, tu serais venu, il serait venu, nous serions venus, vous seriez venu(s), ils seraient venus*

10. *je suis né, tu es né, il est né, nous sommes nés, vous êtes né(s), ils sont nés*

11. *je m'étais habillé, tu t'étais habillé, il s'était habillé, nous nous étions habillés, vous vous étiez habillé(s), ils s'étaient habillés*

12. *je me serai couché, tu te seras couché, il se sera couché, nous nous serons couchés, vous vous serez couché(s), ils se seront couchés*

CHAPTER 10

A.

1. *danse, dansons, dansez*
2. *je finisse, tu finisses, il finisse, nous finissions, vous finissiez, ils finissent*
3. *j'aie vendu, tu aies vendu, il ait vendu, nous ayons vendu, vous ayez vendu, ils aient vendu*
4. *réussis, réussissons, réussissez*
5. *je chante, tu chantes, il chante, nous chantions, vous chantiez, ils chantent*
6. *j'aie étudié, tu aies étudié, il ait étudié, nous ayons étudié, vous ayez étudié, ils aient étudié*
7. *(tu) sois, (nous) soyons, (vous) soyez*
8. *je sache, tu saches, il sache, nous sachions, vous sachiez, ils sachent*
9. *je sois descendu, tu sois descendu, il soit descendu, nous soyons descendus, vous soyez descendu(s), ils soient descendus*
10. *je fasse, tu fasses, il fasse, nous fassions, vous fassiez, ils fassent*

B.

a. *David a bu le jus.*
b. *J'ai lavé mon chat.*

c. *Deux hommes ont construit le balcon.*

d. *La neige recouvre le jardin.*

e. *On a retrouvé votre frère.*

f. *Tout le monde admire son père.*

g. *Ils ont écrit le document hier.*

h. *Des enfants ont acheté ton livre.*

i. *Des meubles remplissent le salon.*

j. *On m'a appelé hier.*

CHAPTER 11

A.

1. *Est-ce que tu aimes les livres ? Aimes-tu les livres ?*

2. *Est-ce qu'il croit tout ? Croit-il tout ?*

3. *Est-ce que vous partirez à midi ? Partirez-vous à midi ?*

4. *Est-ce qu'elles savent la vérité ? Savent-elles la vérité ?*

5. *Est-ce qu'elle aime lire ? Aime-t-elle lire ?*

6. *Est-ce qu'ils parlent français ? Parlent-ils français ?*

7. *Est-ce que nous aimons voyager ? Aimons-nous voyager ?*

8. *Est-ce que vous êtes allés en France ? Êtes-vous allés en France ?*

9. *Est-ce qu'il a mangé avec nous ? A-t-il mangé avec nous ?*

10. *Est-ce qu'elle adore regarder les films ? Adore-t-elle regarder les films ?*

B.

a. *N'est-t-il pas encore arrivé ? Si.*

b. *Ne veux-tu pas manger ? Si.*

c. *Où travaille-t-elle ?*

d. *Pourquoi détestes-tu (détestez-vous) les pommes ?*

e. *Combien de cousins ont-ils ?*

f. *Quel homme a dit bonjour ?*

g. *Qui parle français ?*

h. *Qui as-tu vu ?*

i. *Que veulent-ils ?*

j. *Je veux un chat. Lequel ?*

CHAPTER 12

A.

1. *Je ne parle pas français.*
2. *Il n'a jamais trouvé les livres.*
3. *Je n'aime plus danser.*
4. *N'allez-vous pas étudier ?*
5. *Pas aujourd'hui.*
6. *Je e sais pas.*
7. *Il n'a rien fait.*
8. *Personne ne va le faire ?*
9. *Je n'ai aucune idée.*
10. *Nous ne connaissons pas un seul avocat.*

B.

a. *Oui, je viens.*
b. *Non, il ne nage pas.*
c. *Oui, nous savons.*
d. *Non, David ne vient pas.*
e. *Si, je veux manger.*
f. *Non, nous n'allons pas étudier.*
g. *Si ! Ils vont finir !*
h. *Non, nous n'avons pas encore réussi ?*
i. *Si, je connais un étudiant.*
j. *Non, nous ne pouvons pas aller à la banque.*

CHAPTER 13

A.

1. *Nous allons à la pharmacie.*
2. *C'est un livre de musique.*
3. *Je suis arrivée chez Pierre.*
4. *Qu'est-ce qui est dans la boîte ?*
5. *Je vais avec ma famille.*
6. *Il étudie depuis deux heures.*

7. *Elles ont étudié (pendant) deux heures.*
8. *On va partir à midi.*
9. *Il va en Égypte.*
10. *Nous sommes à Milan.*

B.

a. *aider à*
b. *entrer dans*
c. *oublier de*
d. *penser de*
e. *jouer à*
f. *continuer à / de*
g. *chercher*
h. *commencer à / de*
i. *écouter*
j. *venir de*

CHAPTER 14

A.

1. *Je le cherche.*
2. *Il les veut.*
3. *Nous lui avons écrit.*
4. *Je vais leur parler.*
5. *L'as-tu vu ?*
6. *Ils n'y vont pas.*
7. *En avez-vous beaucoup ?*
8. *Allez-y.*
9. *Cherchons-les.*
10. *Écoutez-la.*

B.

a. *Il les leur achète.*
b. *Nous irons l'y chercher.*
c. *Je vais le lui donner.*

d. *Elle ne veut pas l'y étudier.*

e. *Je lui en ai trouvé.*

f. *Achetez-les y.*

g. *Ne les y mange pas.*

h. *Mettons-l'y.*

i. *Donnez-le-lui.*

j. *Montre-les-leur.*

CHAPTER 15

A.

1. *que*—subordinating conjunction
2. *et*—coordinating conjunction
3. *ce que*—indefinite relative pronoun
4. *ou bien*—coordinating conjunction
5. *parce que*—subordinating conjunction
6. *qui*—relative pronoun
7. *auquel*—relative pronoun
8. *tandis que*—subordinating conjunction
9. *soit, soit*—coordinating conjunction
10. *ce dont*—indefinite relative pronoun

B.

a. *Si tu n'es pas fatigué, raconte-moi une histoire.*

b. *Il chante pendant toute la journée s'il est heureux.*

c. *Si j'étais riche, j'achèterais une voiture.*

d. *Est-ce que nous verrons s'il tombe ?*

e. *Si elle me donnait de l'argent, je voyagerais.*

f. *Il ne pourrait pas dormir s'il faisait chaud.*

g. *S'ils avaient été prêts, nous serions partis.*

h. *Sa mère téléphonerait si Michel était malade.*

i. *Si tu avais voulu étudier, tu aurais dû le leur dire.*

j. *Ils me l'auraient dit s'ils avaient voulu venir.*

CHAPTER 16

A.

1. *admirablement*
2. *passionnément*
3. *naturellement*
4. *premièrement*
5. *vivement*
6. *intelligemment*
7. *bruyamment*
8. *patiemment*
9. *confortablement*
10. *spontanément*

B.

a. *Tu parles beaucoup.*
b. *Il est déjà sorti.*
c. *Je vais rarement en France.*
d. *Il y a trop de bruit.*
e. *La plupart des étudiants sont prêts.*
f. *Thomas est aussi grand que Pierre.*
g. *Ce livre est moins intéressant.*
h. *Lise est la fille la plus intelligente.*
i. *Voici une meilleure idée.*

CHAPTER 17

A.

1. *C'est une idée intéressante.*
2. *Elle est très chic.*
3. *À vous parler franc . . .*
4. *Préférez-vous la chemise verte ou la chemise bleu clair ?*
5. *J'ai vu deux films étrangers la semaine passée.*
6. *Il porte des chaussures blanches et noires / blanc et noir.*
7. *Je cherche une boucherie kascher.*

8. *Ils travaillent dur.*
9. *Elle a des cheveux auburn.*
10. *Nous cherchons une ceinture vert foncé.*

B.

a. *Hélène s'est levée à huit heures.*
b. *Nous sommes allés à la banque.*
c. *Voici les clés qu'il a perdues.*
d. *Elles sont sorties hier soir.*
e. *Cette femme est très respectée.*
f. *Les lampes que Lise a achetées ne marchent pas.*
g. *Ils se sont réveillés trop tard.*
h. *Où est la table que nous avons vue hier ?*
i. *Les meubles seront refaits jeudi.*
j. *Élisabeth, t'es-tu lavé les mains ?*

CHAPTER 18

A.

1. *Le restaurant est fermé ? C'est difficile à croire.*
2. *Cet homme-là, il est avocat.*
3. *C'est nous qui allons en France.*
4. *Ma soeur, c'est une artiste.*
5. *Ce musée, est très intéressant.*
6. *Voici David. Il est étudiant en histoire.*
7. *Qui est à la porte ? C'est Lise.*
8. *Elle est actrice.*
9. *Je vois tes livres, ils sont sur la table.*
10. *C'est mon ami qui l'a fait.*

B.

a. *Il y a un homme dans votre bureau.*
b. *Il y avait cinq étudiants.*
c. *Nous l'avons vue il y a une semaine.*
d. *Qu'est-ce qu'il y a ?*

e. *Combien de tables y a-t-il ?*

f. *Il n'y a pas de tables.*

g. *Il y aura un examen demain.*

h. *J'ai mangé il y a une heure.*

i. *Y a-t-il du pain ? Est-ce qu'il y a du pain ?*

j. *Non, il n'y pas de pain.*

CHAPTER 19

A.

1. *Voici mes livres.*
2. *Le père de Michel est médecin.*
3. *Je cherche tes / vos clés.*
4. *Quel est son restaurant préféré ?*
5. *Je n'aime pas les idées du professeur.*
6. Leurs *amis sont très sympas.*
7. *Les voitures des étudiants doivent être fermées à clé.*
8. *Notre maison est là-bas.*
9. *C'est mon actrice préférée.*
10. *Voilà ma* mère *et* mon *père.*

B.

a. *C'est le mien. Il à moi.*

b. *Voici les nôtres.*

c. *La voiture est à lui. Elle est à lui. C'est la sienne.*

d. *J'aime les tiennes.*

e. *Ce sont les nôtres. Ces documents sont à nous.*

f. *Cet étudiant est dans la sienne. Cet étudiant dans sa classe.*

g. *Les livres sont pour eux/ Ils sont pour eux.*

h. *C'est la nôtre ou la vôtre.*

i. *Où est la mienne ?*

j. *La leur est très petite.*

Further Reading

The Everything French Grammar Book provides an overview of French grammar. Here are some recommended resources for further information.

About the French Language, by Laura K. Lawless
✑*http://french.about.com*
Web site with lessons on every aspect of the French language, including grammar, vocabulary, verb tables, sound files, and a special section for beginning students.

The Everything French Verb Book, by Laura K. Lawless
Avon, MA: Adams Media Corporation, 2005
Introductory French verb lessons plus 250 verb tables.

The Everything French Phrase Book, by Laura K. Lawless
Avon, MA: Adams Media Corporation, 2005
French vocabulary and phrases for all types of travel situations.

À l'écoute de la langue française
✑*www.frenchclasses.com/french/cdrom*
French learning program with gradual immersion in French.

Bibliography

The American Heritage Dictionary of the English Language, (Boston, MA: Houghton Mifflin Company, 2000).

Ethnologue Report: ✐*www.ethnologue.com/show_language .asp?code=FRN*

French is Not a "Foreign" Language!, American Association of Teachers of French. (pamphlet)

Rapport sur l'état de la Francophonie dans le monde. Données 1997/98 et six études inédites. Haut Conseil de la Francophonie, Paris, la Documentation française, 1999.

Rhodes, N. C., & Branaman, L. E. "Foreign language instruction in the United States: A national survey of elementary and secondary schools." Center for Applied Linguistics and Delta Systems, 1999.

United States Census, Ten Languages Most Frequently Spoken at Home Other than English and Spanish: 2000, figure 3 : ✐*www .census.gov/prod/2003pubs/c2kbr-29.pdf*

Weber, George. "The World's 10 Most Influential Languages," *Language Today*, Vol. 2, Dec 1997.

Index